11

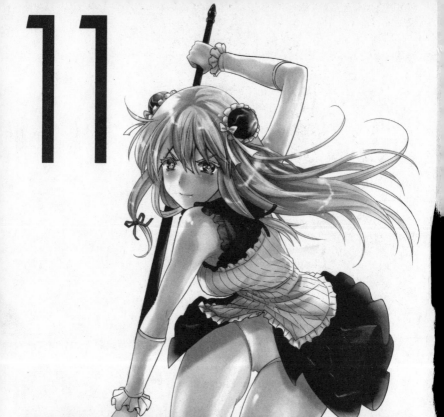

PARALLEL PARADISE

story and art
LYNN OKAMOTO

C O N T E N T S

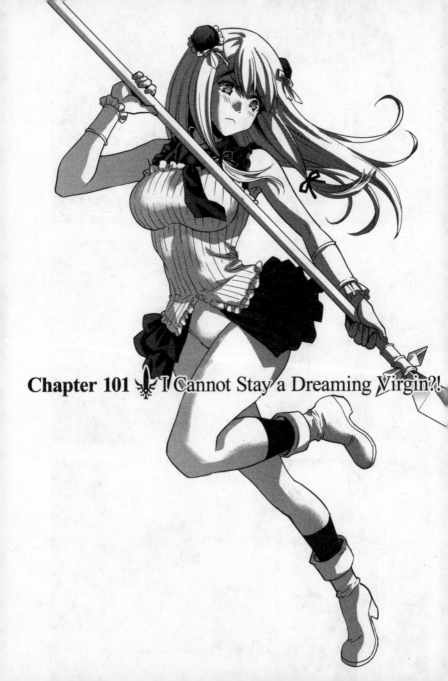

Chapter 101 ✦ I Cannot Stay a Dreaming Virgin?!

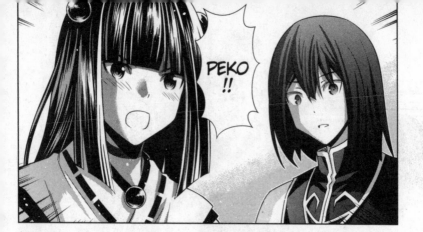

PEKO!!

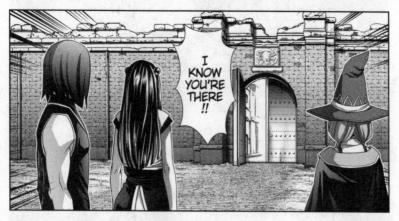

I KNOW YOU'RE THERE!!

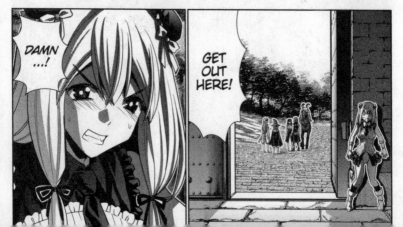

DAMN...!

GET OUT HERE!

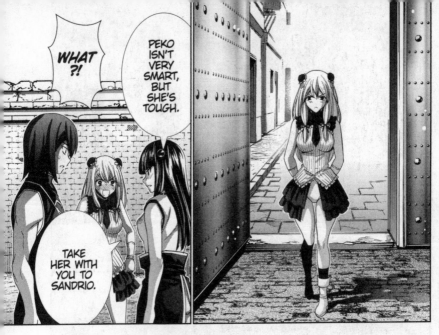

WHAT?!

PEKO ISN'T VERY SMART, BUT SHE'S TOUGH.

TAKE HER WITH YOU TO SANDRIO.

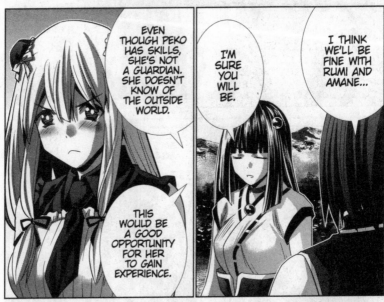

EVEN THOUGH PEKO HAS SKILLS, SHE'S NOT A GUARDIAN. SHE DOESN'T KNOW OF THE OUTSIDE WORLD.

THIS WOULD BE A GOOD OPPORTUNITY FOR HER TO GAIN EXPERIENCE.

I'M SURE YOU WILL BE.

I THINK WE'LL BE FINE WITH RUMI AND AMANE...

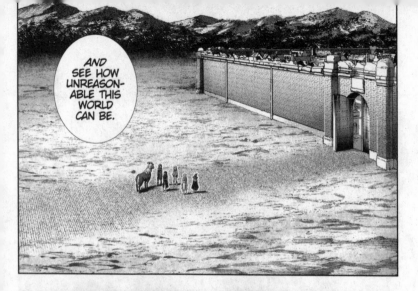

AND SEE HOW UNREASONABLE THIS WORLD CAN BE.

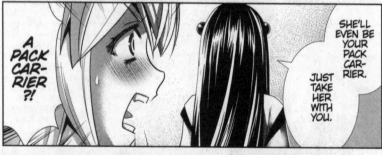

A PACK CARRIER?!

SHE'LL EVEN BE YOUR PACK CARRIER.

JUST TAKE HER WITH YOU.

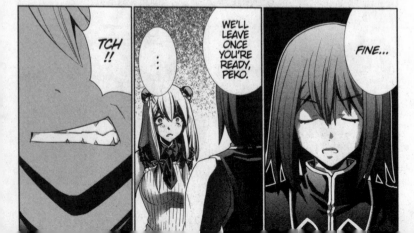

TCH!!

...

WE'LL LEAVE ONCE YOU'RE READY, PEKO.

FINE...

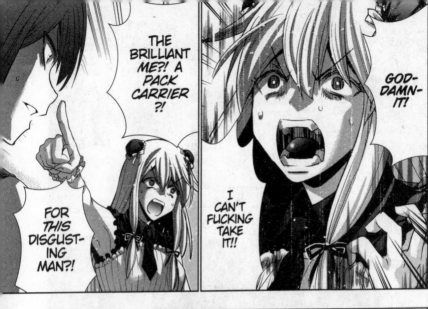

THE BRILLIANT ME?! A PACK CARRIER?!

FOR *THIS* DISGUSTING MAN?!

GOD-DAMN-IT!

I CAN'T FUCKING TAKE IT!!

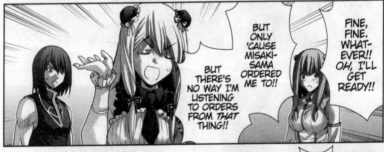

BUT ONLY 'CAUSE MISAKI-SAMA ORDERED ME TO!!

BUT THERE'S NO WAY I'M LISTENING TO ORDERS FROM *THAT* THING!!

FINE, FINE, WHAT-EVER!! OH, I'LL GET READY!!

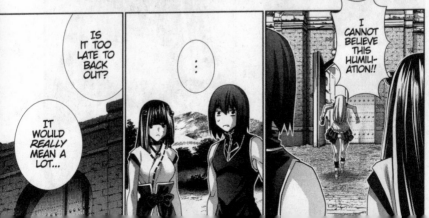

IS IT TOO LATE TO BACK OUT?

IT WOULD *REALLY* MEAN A LOT...

⋮

I CANNOT BELIEVE THIS HUMILI-ATION!!

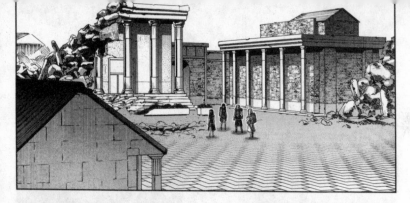

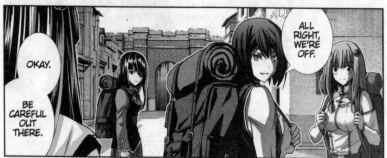

OKAY.

BE CAREFUL OUT THERE.

ALL RIGHT, WE'RE OFF.

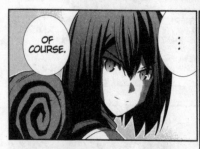

OF COURSE.

⋮

I KNOW YOU'LL RELEASE THE HUMANS FROM THEIR LAST MOON ...

AND DEFEAT THE JEALOUS GOD.

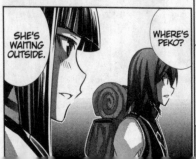

SHE'S WAITING OUTSIDE.

WHERE'S PEKO?

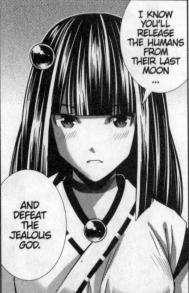

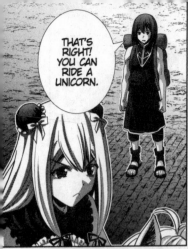

THAT'S RIGHT! YOU CAN RIDE A UNICORN.

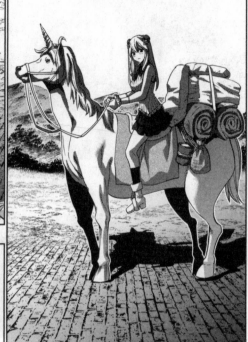

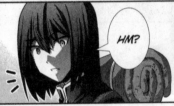

HM?

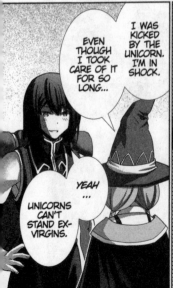

EVEN THOUGH I TOOK CARE OF IT FOR SO LONG...

I WAS KICKED BY THE UNICORN. I'M IN SHOCK.

YEAH...

UNICORNS CAN'T STAND EX-VIRGINS.

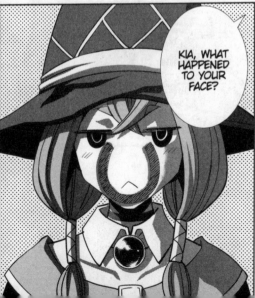

KIA, WHAT HAPPENED TO YOUR FACE?

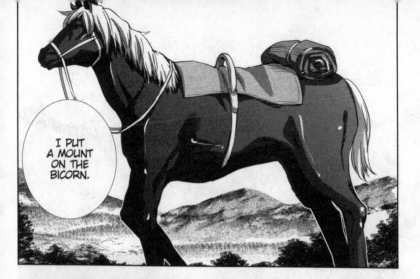

I PUT A MOUNT ON THE BICORN.

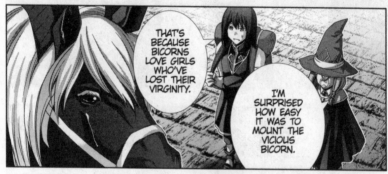

THAT'S BECAUSE BICORNS LOVE GIRLS WHO'VE LOST THEIR VIRGINITY.

I'M SURPRISED HOW EASY IT WAS TO MOUNT THE VICIOUS BICORN.

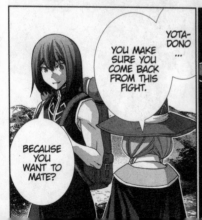

YOTA-DONO...

YOU MAKE SURE YOU COME BACK FROM THIS FIGHT.

BECAUSE YOU WANT TO MATE?

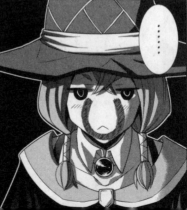

......

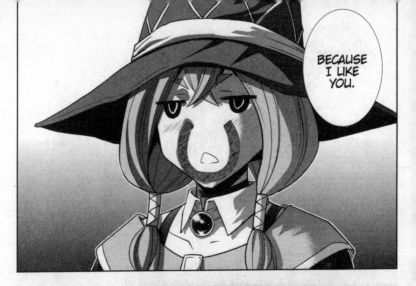

BECAUSE I LIKE YOU.

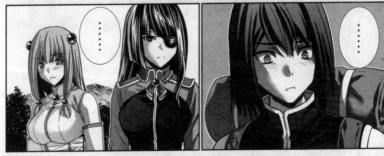

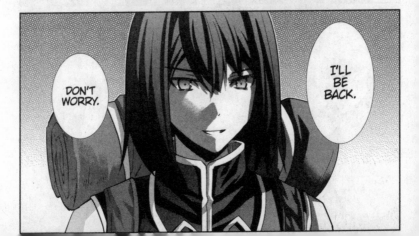

DON'T WORRY.

I'LL BE BACK.

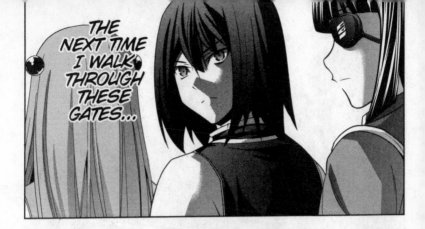

THE NEXT TIME I WALK THROUGH THESE GATES...

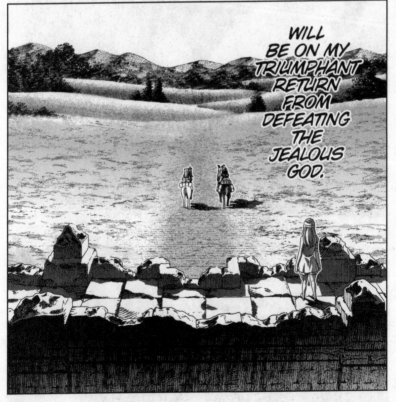

WILL BE ON MY TRIUMPHANT RETURN FROM DEFEATING THE JEALOUS GOD.

LET'S GO!!
REAR
HIYAH !!
WAHH !!
KA-KLUCK
KA-KLUCK
TOO FAST!! TOO FAST!!
KA-KLUCK
ARE YOU SURE WE SHOULD BE GOING THIS FAST?!
IF IT'S LIKE A UNICORN, IT SHOULD BE NO PROB-LEM!!
KA-KLUCK

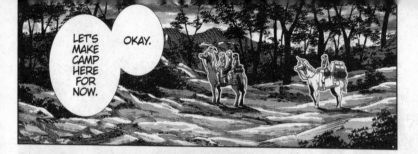

LET'S MAKE CAMP HERE FOR NOW.

OKAY.

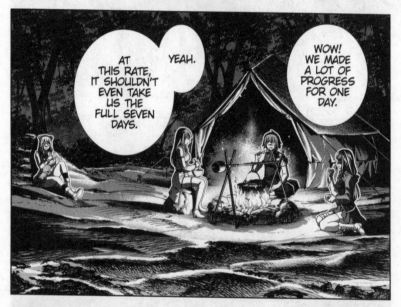

AT THIS RATE, IT SHOULDN'T EVEN TAKE US THE FULL SEVEN DAYS.

YEAH.

WOW! WE MADE A LOT OF PROGRESS FOR ONE DAY.

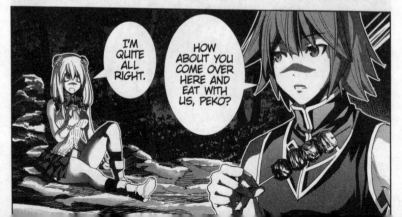

I'M QUITE ALL RIGHT.

HOW ABOUT YOU COME OVER HERE AND EAT WITH US, PEKO?

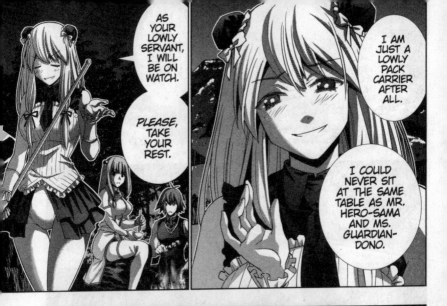

AS YOUR LOWLY SERVANT, I WILL BE ON WATCH.

PLEASE, TAKE YOUR REST.

I AM JUST A LOWLY PACK CARRIER AFTER ALL.

I COULD NEVER SIT AT THE SAME TABLE AS MR. HERO-SAMA AND MS. GUARDIAN-DONO.

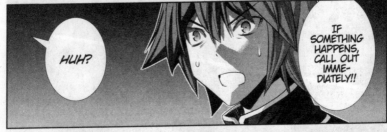

HUH?

IF SOMETHING HAPPENS, CALL OUT IMME-DIATELY!!

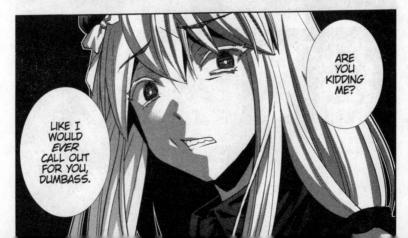

ARE YOU KIDDING ME?

LIKE I WOULD *EVER* CALL OUT FOR YOU, DUMBASS.

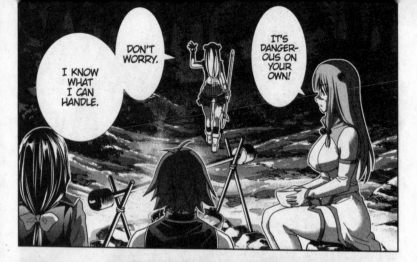

I KNOW WHAT I CAN HANDLE.

DON'T WORRY.

IT'S DANGEROUS ON YOUR OWN!

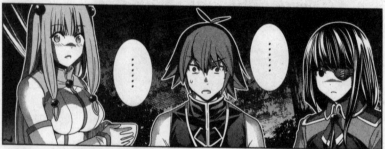

. . . .

. . . .

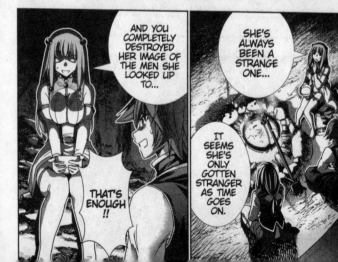

AND YOU COMPLETELY DESTROYED HER IMAGE OF THE MEN SHE LOOKED UP TO...

THAT'S ENOUGH!!

SHE'S ALWAYS BEEN A STRANGE ONE...

WHAT'S HER PROBLEM?

IT SEEMS SHE'S ONLY GOTTEN STRANGER AS TIME GOES ON.

WSSSK
ホーーッ
WSSSK
ホーーッ
WSSSK
ホーーッ
WSSSK
ホーーッ
スーーッ
ZZZZ
スーーッ
ZZZZ
...
TCH!

RUSTLE
RUSTLE
WHO THE HELL'S IDEA WAS IT TO PUT A TENT HERE?!

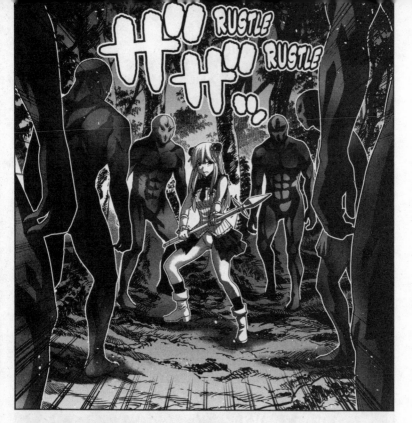

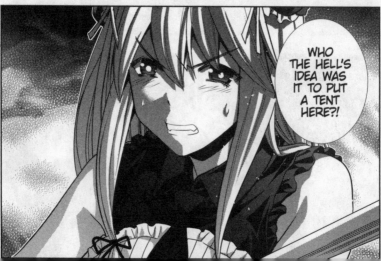

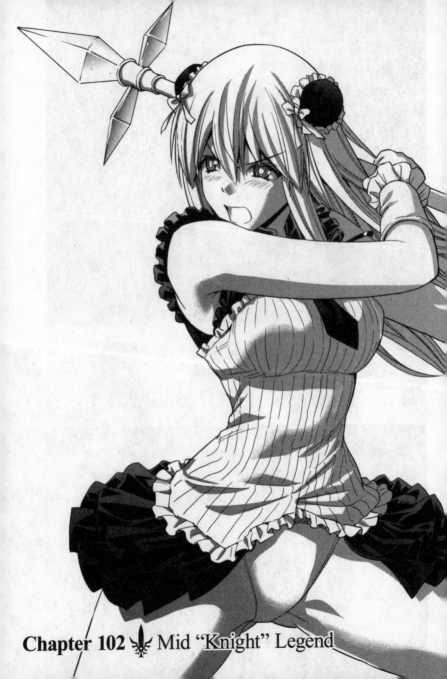

Chapter 102 Mid "Knight" Legend

......
RUSTLE
HEH HEH HEH ...
ONE... TWO...
THREE... FOUR...
FIVE... SIX...
SEVEN... EIGHT.
ONE-ON-EIGHT, HUH...

NOT EVEN CLOSE TO ENOUGH.
THUUUD

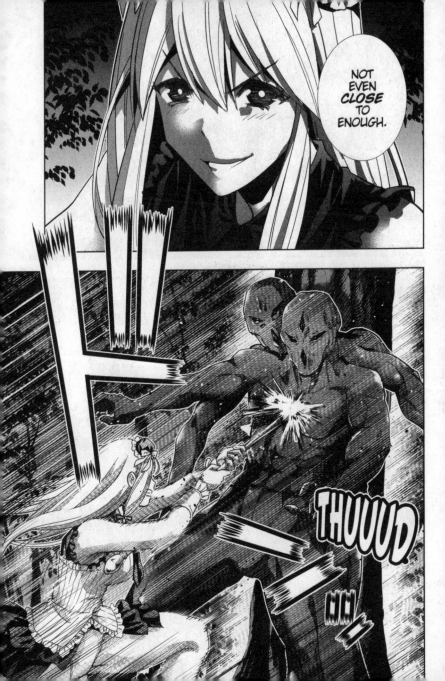

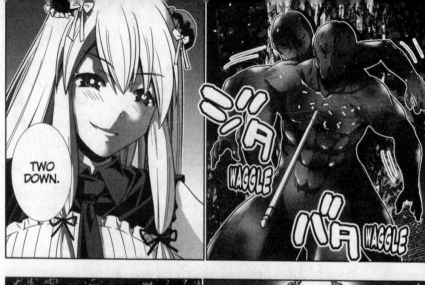

TWO
DOWN.

ジタ
WAGGLE

バタ
WAGGLE

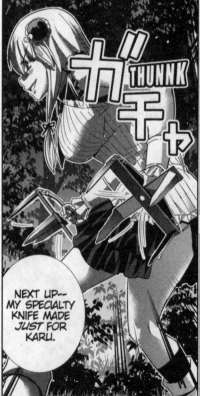

ガチャ
THUNNK

NEXT UP--
MY SPECIALTY
KNIFE MADE
JUST FOR
KARU.

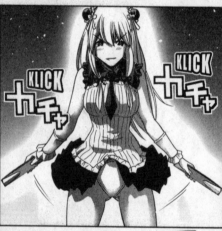

KLICK
カチャ

KLICK
カチャ

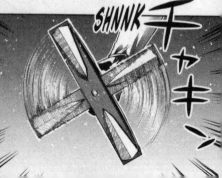

SHNNK
チャキン

WHUMP
FSHHHHHHHH
AND THAT'S FOUR DOWN.
FU FU FU... WITH THIS THING, THE KARU ARE NOTHING BUT WALKING TOFU.

WHAM
FSHHHH
NOW, NOW.
YOU DIDN'T EVEN BOTHER HIDING YOUR PRESENCE!
WHUMP
WHAM

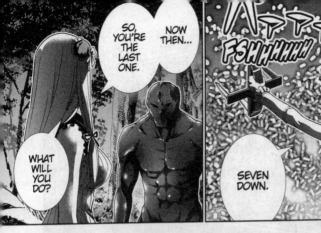

SO, YOU'RE THE LAST ONE.

NOW THEN...

WHAT WILL YOU DO?

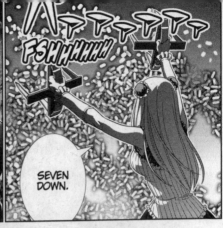

FSHHHHHH

SEVEN DOWN.

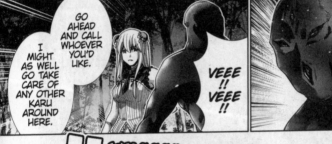

I MIGHT AS WELL GO TAKE CARE OF ANY OTHER KARU AROUND HERE.

GO AHEAD AND CALL WHOEVER YOU'D LIKE.

VEEE!! VEEE!!

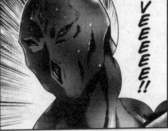

VEEEEEE!!

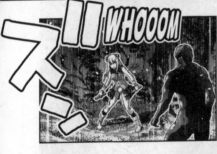

WHOOOM

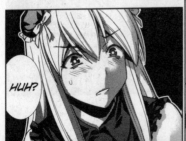

HUH?

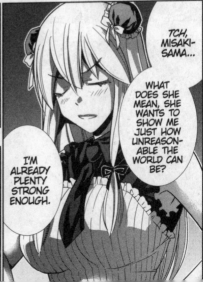

TCH, MISAKI-SAMA...

WHAT DOES SHE MEAN, SHE WANTS TO SHOW ME JUST HOW UNREASONABLE THE WORLD CAN BE?

I'M ALREADY PLENTY STRONG ENOUGH.

ズン
WHOOM
バキバキ
KRACK KRACK
ズン
WHOOM

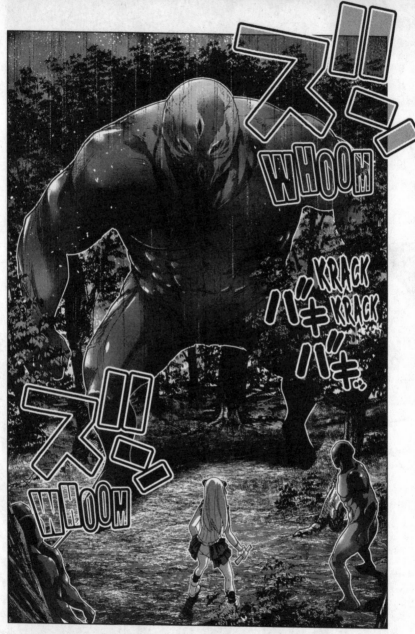

WHOOM
ズ
WHOOM
ズ
HSHHHHH!
SERI-OUSLY...
S-SORRY...
MAYBE THE WORLD IS A LITTLE LARGER THAN I THOUGHT...

ザッ
RUSTLE
ザッ
RUSTLE
?!
TCH!
WHOOM

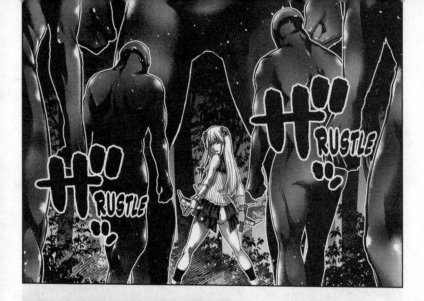

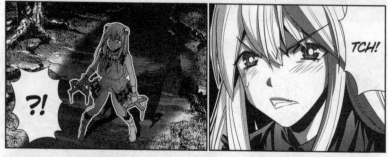

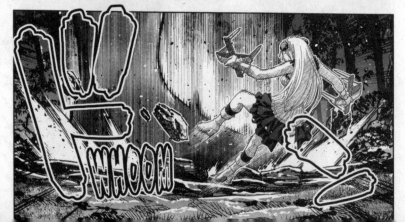

THHHNK
ズ…
THERE IS A ONE IN FOUR CHANCE I'LL HIT THE RIGHT SPOT...
ドッ
WHUMP
TAKE THAT !!

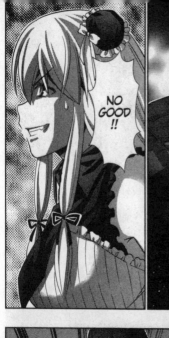

NO GOOD !!

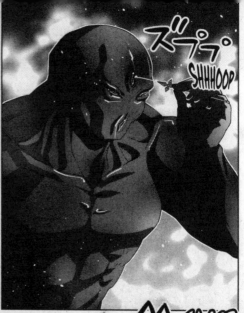

ズプフ
SHHHOOP

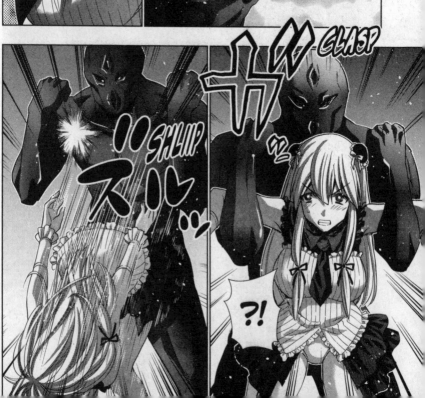

カッ
カッ

クラスプ
CLASP

SHLIIP
ズルッ

?!

WHAM
WHAM
CLASP
CREEEAK
CREEAK
CREAK
AHHHHH!!

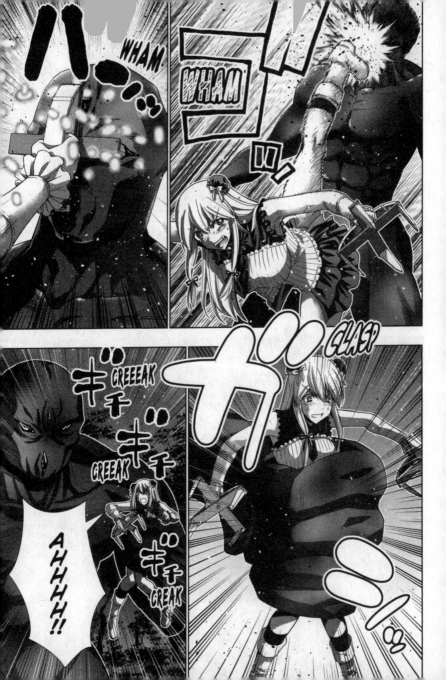

SPLIT
VEEEEE!!
VEEEEE!!
RIIIP
RIIIP

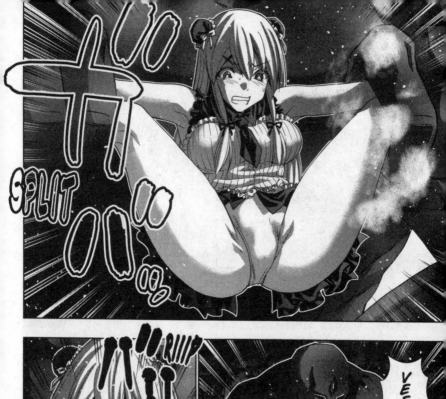

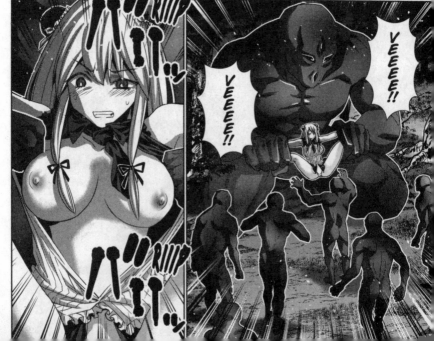

HACK
GET OFF ME!!
WHAM
WHAM
RIIIIP

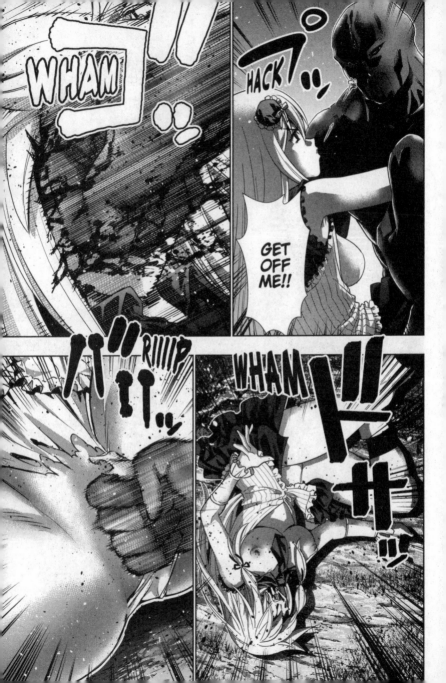

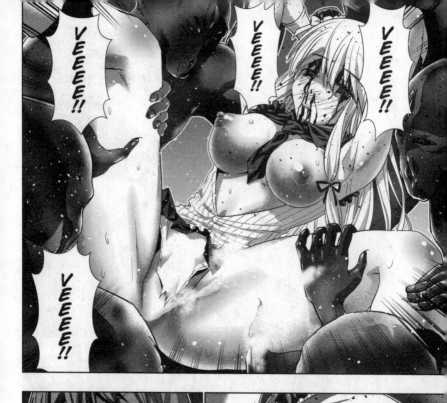

VEEEE!!

VEEEE!!

VEEEE!!

VEEEE!!

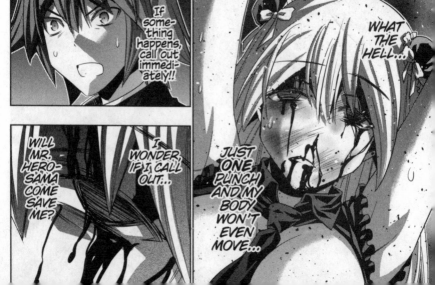

If something happens, call out immediately!!

WHAT THE HELL...

WILL MR. HERO-SAMA COME SAVE ME?

I WONDER, IF I CALL OUT...

JUST ONE PUNCH AND MY BODY WON'T EVEN MOVE...

WAS ALL MY TRAINING AND WORK FOR NOTHING ...?
VEEEEE!!
VEEEEE!!
VEEEEE!!
NO MATTER HOW STRONG I AM...IF I GET PUNCHED ONCE, I'M DONE. THEN I DIE, NOTHING MORE THAN A TARGET OF THEIR LUST...
VEEEEE!!
UNBELIEV-ABLE...
HAVE I ALWAYS BEEN THIS WEAK ...?
CLENCH
UGH ...

HELP ME...

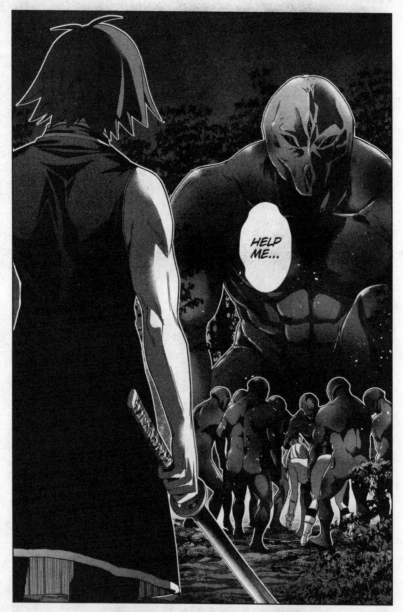

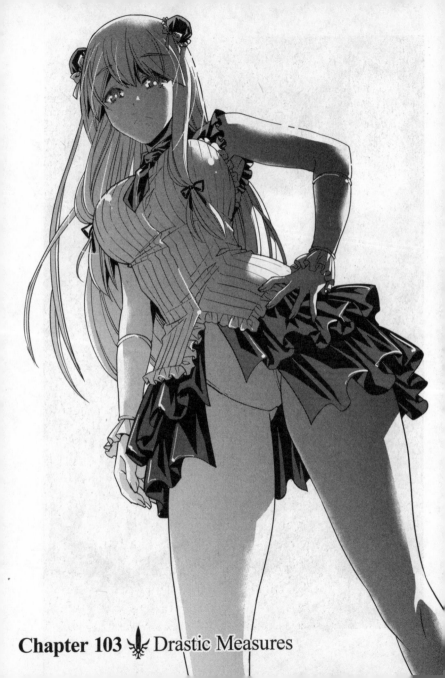

Chapter 103 Drastic Measures

VEEEEEE!!
VEEEEE!!
VEEEEE!!
HEL...

KSHH
KSHH

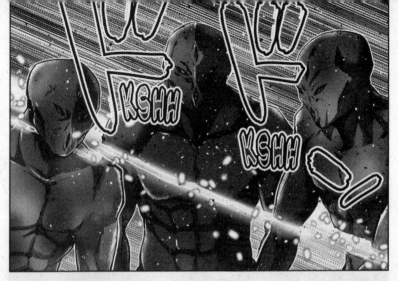

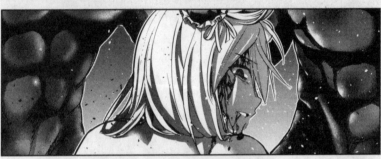

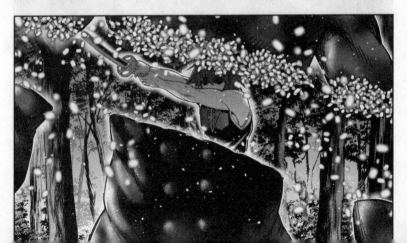

ドッ
THUD
ドッ
THUD
YOU WAITED TOO LONG TO CALL ME.
DUMMY.
?!
?!
?!

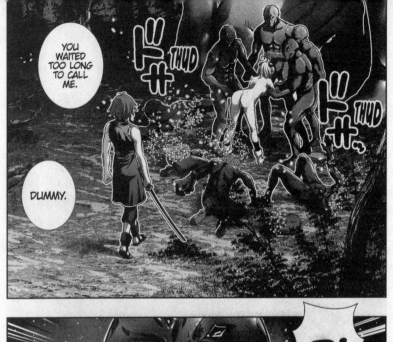

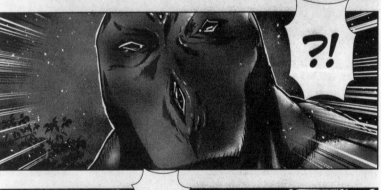

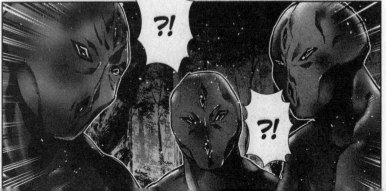

VEEEEEE!!
WHOOM
WHOOM
VEEEEEE!!
VEEEEEE!!
VEEEEEE!!
VEEEEEE!!
......
WHAT?

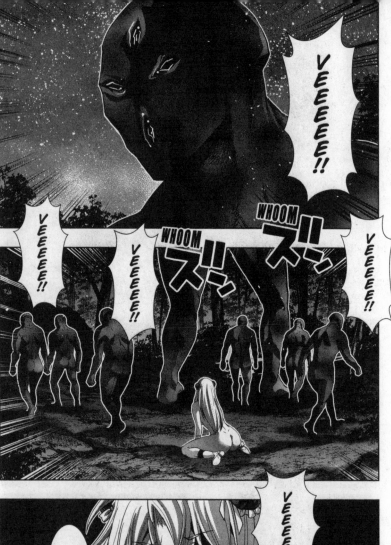

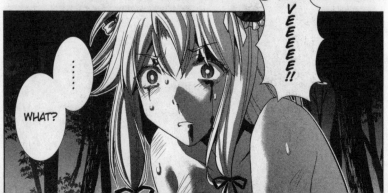

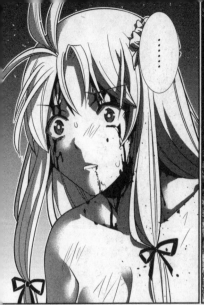

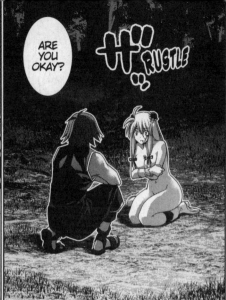

ARE YOU OKAY?

ザザ RUSTLE

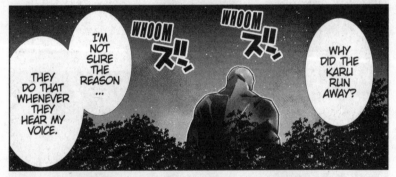

I'M NOT SURE THE REASON...

THEY DO THAT WHENEVER THEY HEAR MY VOICE.

WHOOM ズン

WHOOM ズン

WHY DID THE KARU RUN AWAY?

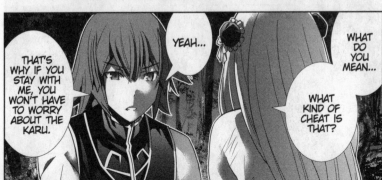

THAT'S WHY IF YOU STAY WITH ME, YOU WON'T HAVE TO WORRY ABOUT THE KARU.

YEAH...

WHAT DO YOU MEAN...

WHAT KIND OF CHEAT IS THAT?

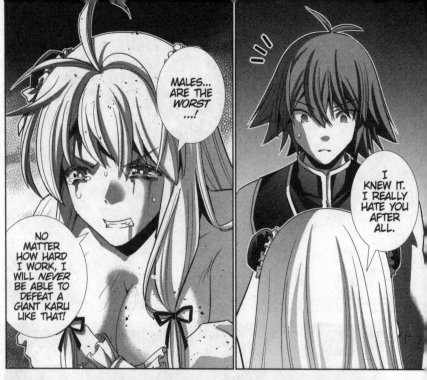

MALES... ARE THE *WORST* ....!

NO MATTER HOW HARD I WORK, I WILL *NEVER* BE ABLE TO DEFEAT A GIANT KARU LIKE THAT!

I KNEW IT. I REALLY HATE YOU AFTER ALL.

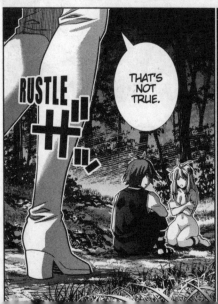

RUSTLE

THAT'S NOT TRUE.

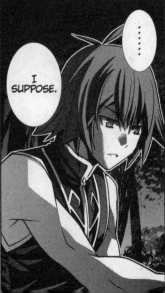

......

I SUPPOSE.

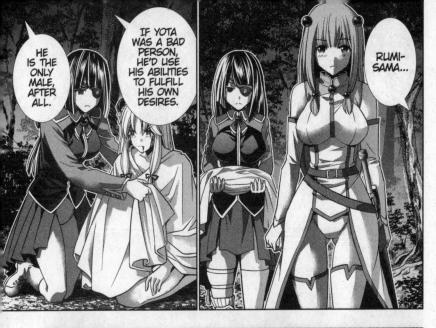

HE IS THE ONLY MALE, AFTER ALL.

IF YOTA WAS A BAD PERSON, HE'D USE HIS ABILITIES TO FULFILL HIS OWN DESIRES.

RUMI-SAMA...

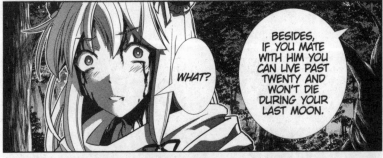

WHAT?

BESIDES, IF YOU MATE WITH HIM YOU CAN LIVE PAST TWENTY AND WON'T DIE DURING YOUR LAST MOON.

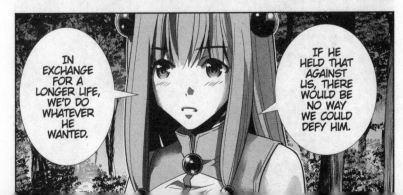

IN EXCHANGE FOR A LONGER LIFE, WE'D DO WHATEVER HE WANTED.

IF HE HELD THAT AGAINST US, THERE WOULD BE NO WAY WE COULD DEFY HIM.

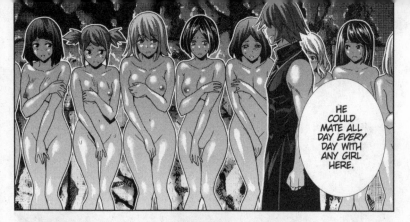

HE COULD MATE ALL DAY *EVERY* DAY WITH ANY GIRL HERE.

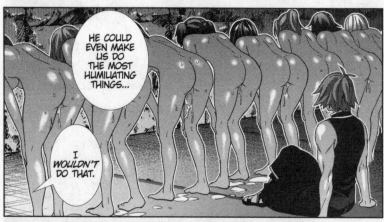

HE COULD EVEN MAKE US DO THE MOST HUMILIATING THINGS...

I *WOULDN'T* DO THAT.

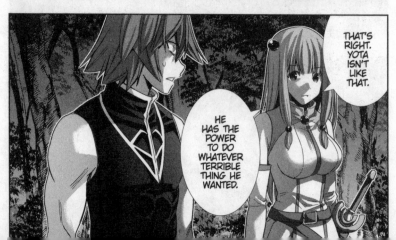

THAT'S RIGHT. YOTA ISN'T LIKE THAT.

HE HAS THE POWER TO DO WHATEVER TERRIBLE THING HE WANTED.

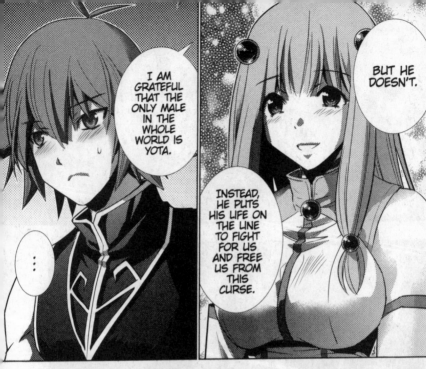

I AM GRATEFUL THAT THE ONLY MALE IN THE WHOLE WORLD IS YOTA.

...

BUT HE DOESN'T.

INSTEAD, HE PUTS HIS LIFE ON THE LINE TO FIGHT FOR US AND FREE US FROM THIS CURSE.

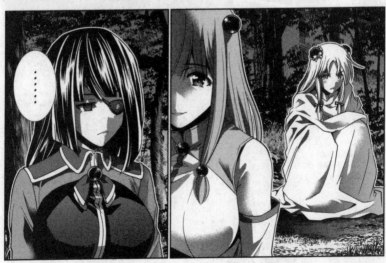

...

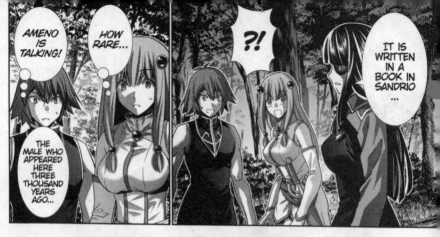

AMENO IS TALKING!

HOW RARE...

?!

IT IS WRITTEN IN A BOOK IN SANDRIO...

THE MALE WHO APPEARED HERE THREE THOUSAND YEARS AGO...

?!

COMMITTED THE MOST TREACHEROUS OF ACTS.

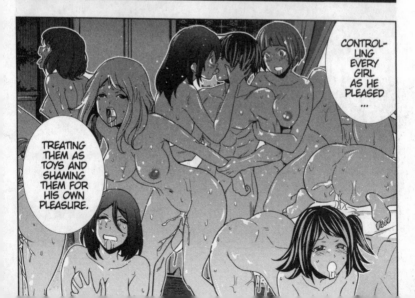

CONTROLLING EVERY GIRL AS HE PLEASED...

TREATING THEM AS TOYS AND SHAMING THEM FOR HIS OWN PLEASURE.

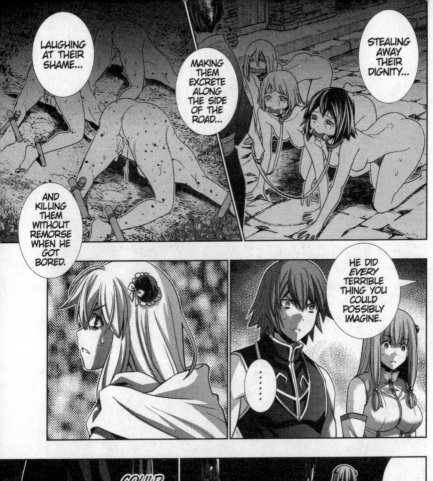

LAUGHING AT THEIR SHAME...

MAKING THEM EXCRETE ALONG THE SIDE OF THE ROAD...

STEALING AWAY THEIR DIGNITY...

AND KILLING THEM WITHOUT REMORSE WHEN HE GOT BORED.

HE DID *EVERY* TERRIBLE THING YOU COULD POSSIBLY IMAGINE.

......

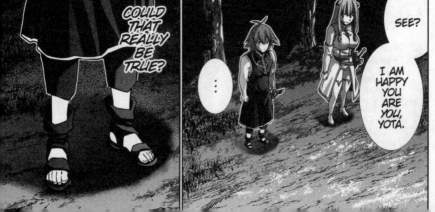

COULD THAT REALLY BE TRUE?

...

SEE?

I AM HAPPY YOU ARE *YOU*, YOTA.

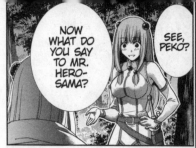

NOW WHAT DO YOU SAY TO MR. HERO-SAMA?

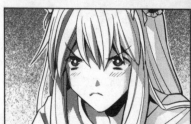

SEE, PEKO?

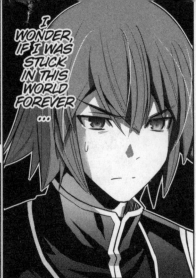

I WONDER, IF I WAS STUCK IN THIS WORLD FOREVER...

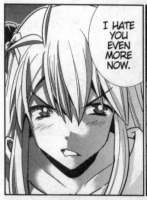

I HATE YOU EVEN MORE NOW.

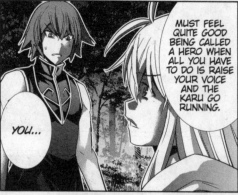

YOU...

MUST FEEL QUITE GOOD BEING CALLED A HERO WHEN ALL YOU HAVE TO DO IS RAISE YOUR VOICE AND THE KARU GO RUNNING.

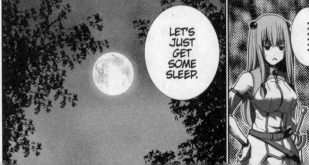

LET'S JUST GET SOME SLEEP.

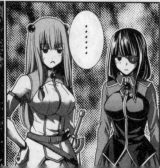

......

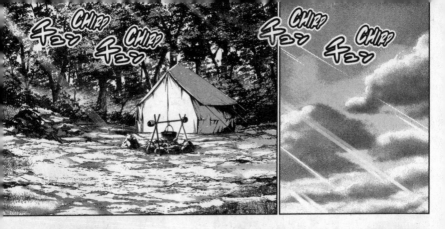

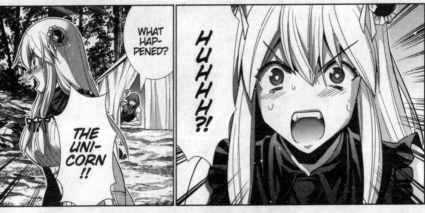

WHAT HAP-PENED?

THE UNI-CORN !!

HUHHH?!

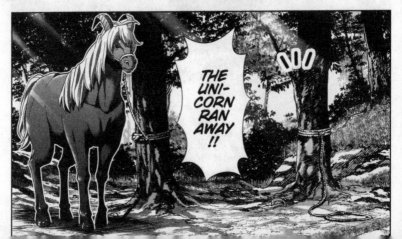

THE UNI-CORN RAN AWAY !!

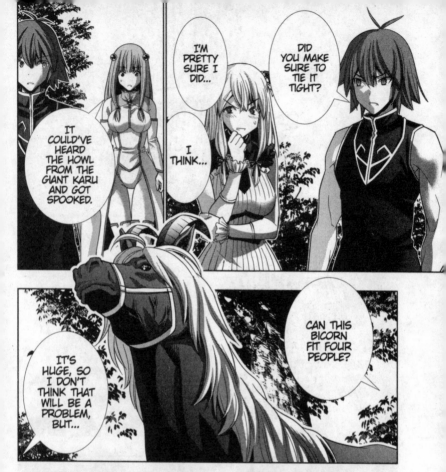

IT COULD'VE HEARD THE HOWL FROM THE GIANT KARU AND GOT SPOOKED.

I THINK...

I'M PRETTY SURE I DID...

DID YOU MAKE SURE TO TIE IT TIGHT?

IT'S HUGE, SO I DON'T THINK THAT WILL BE A PROBLEM, BUT...

CAN THIS BICORN FIT FOUR PEOPLE?

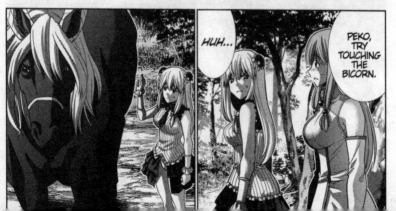

HUH...

PEKO, TRY TOUCHING THE BICORN.

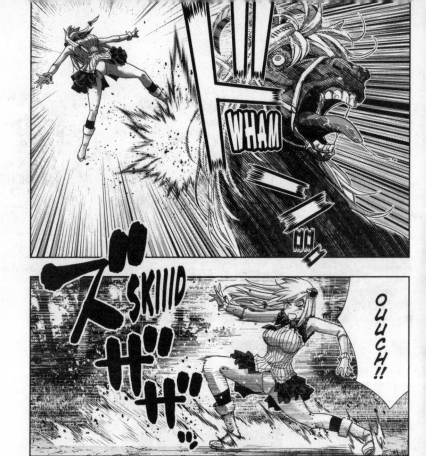

WHAM

SKIIIID

OUUCH!!

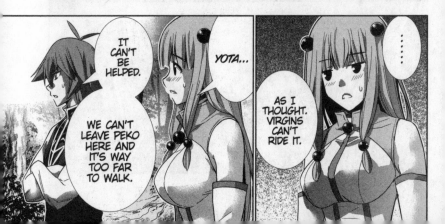

IT CAN'T BE HELPED.

YOTA...

....

WE CAN'T LEAVE PEKO HERE AND IT'S WAY TOO FAR TO WALK.

AS I THOUGHT. VIRGINS CAN'T RIDE IT.

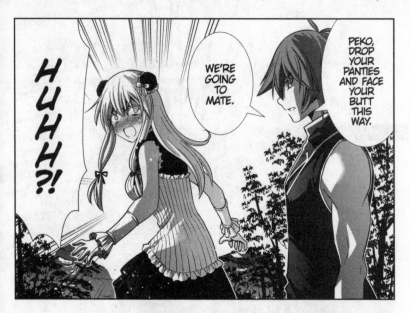

PEKO, DROP YOUR PANTIES AND FACE YOUR BUTT THIS WAY.

WE'RE GOING TO MATE.

HUHH?!

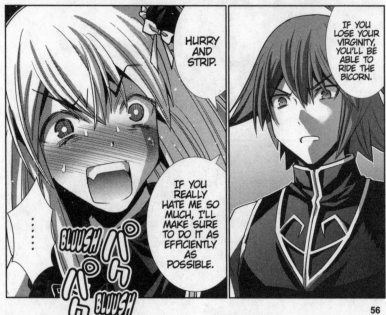

IF YOU LOSE YOUR VIRGINITY, YOU'LL BE ABLE TO RIDE THE BICORN.

HURRY AND STRIP.

IF YOU REALLY HATE ME SO MUCH, I'LL MAKE SURE TO DO IT AS EFFICIENTLY AS POSSIBLE.

......

BLUUSH

BLUUSH

56

Chapter 104 A Secret Forming

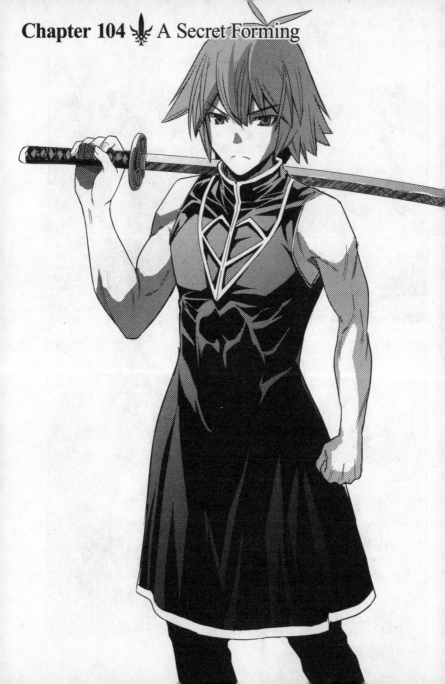

I'LL MATE WITH YOU.
WHAT ?!
DON'T WORRY, I'LL TREAT IT AS A JOB.
NOW HURRY UP AND TAKE YOUR PANTIES OFF AND POINT YOUR REAR THIS WAY.
JUST ONE THRUST AND YOU CAN RIDE THE BICORN.
...
WHO THE HELL DO YOU THINK YOU ARE?
HUH?

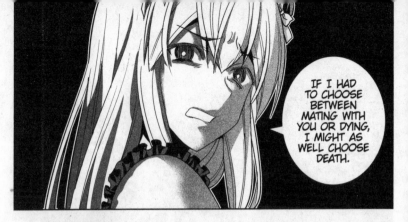

IF I HAD TO CHOOSE BETWEEN MATING WITH YOU OR DYING, I MIGHT AS WELL CHOOSE DEATH.

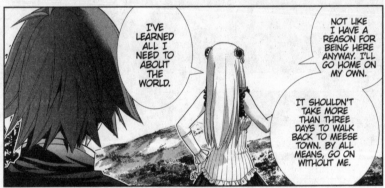

I'VE LEARNED ALL I NEED TO ABOUT THE WORLD.

NOT LIKE I HAVE A REASON FOR BEING HERE ANYWAY. I'LL GO HOME ON MY OWN.

IT SHOULDN'T TAKE MORE THAN THREE DAYS TO WALK BACK TO MEESE TOWN. BY ALL MEANS, GO ON WITHOUT ME.

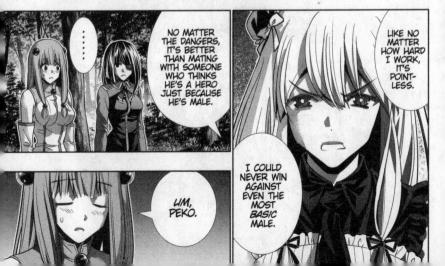

・・・・・・

NO MATTER THE DANGERS, IT'S BETTER THAN MATING WITH SOMEONE WHO THINKS HE'S A HERO JUST BECAUSE HE'S MALE.

LIKE NO MATTER HOW HARD I WORK, IT'S POINTLESS.

UM, PEKO.

I COULD NEVER WIN AGAINST EVEN THE MOST BASIC MALE.

IF WHAT YOU'RE SAYING IS TRUE, THEN WHY ARE YOU SO EXCITED?
?!
にゅるにゅる
DRIBBLE DRIBBLE
HUH ?!
WE UNDERSTAND, PEKO...
WE'VE BEEN DOWN THIS ROAD BEFORE.
WHOOM
BLUUUUSH
YOU'RE TURNED ON BY THE THOUGHT OF MATING WITH YOTA, RIGHT?
......
YOU'RE WRONG ...!!
YOU DON'T NEED TO FIGHT IT.
ALSO, I ALREADY KNOW...

ABOUT THE NUMEROUS PICTURES OF NAKED MEN YOU HAVE.
HUH?!
HOW?!
IT'S QUITE WELL KNOWN.
YOU HAVE A ROOM FULL OF THOSE PICTURES ON THE WALL.
かぁ〜っ
BLUUUSH
YOU DIDN'T KNOW?
......
YOU'RE INTER-ESTED IN MEN, RIGHT?
IT'S NOT YOUR FAULT.

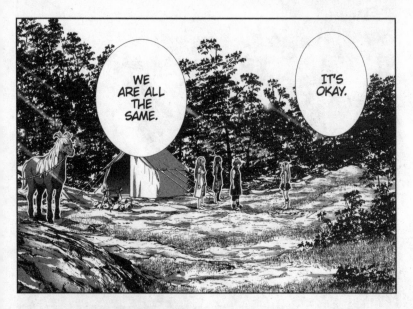

WE ARE ALL THE SAME.

IT'S OKAY.

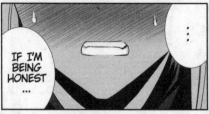

IF I'M BEING HONEST...

:

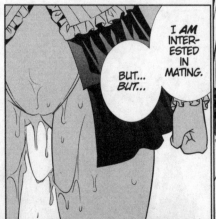

I *AM* INTERESTED IN MATING.

BUT... BUT...

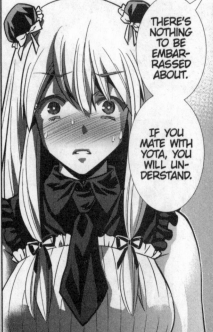

THERE'S NOTHING TO BE EMBARRASSED ABOUT.

IF YOU MATE WITH YOTA, YOU WILL UNDERSTAND.

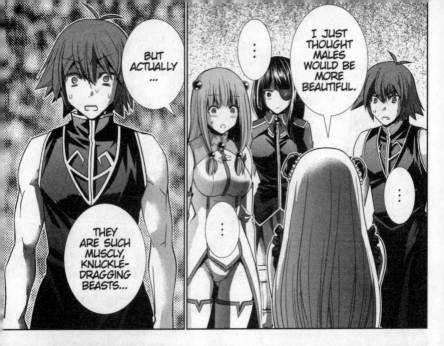

BUT ACTUALLY...

THEY ARE SUCH MUSCLY, KNUCKLE-DRAGGING BEASTS...

...

I JUST THOUGHT MALES WOULD BE MORE BEAUTIFUL.

...

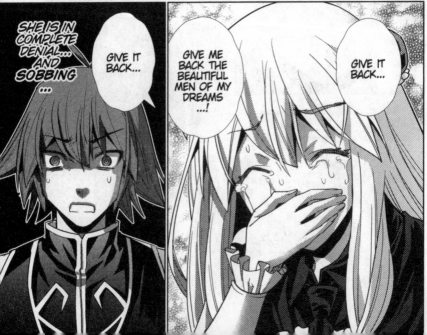

SHE IS IN COMPLETE DENIAL... AND SOBBING...

GIVE IT BACK...

GIVE ME BACK THE BEAUTIFUL MEN OF MY DREAMS...!

GIVE IT BACK...

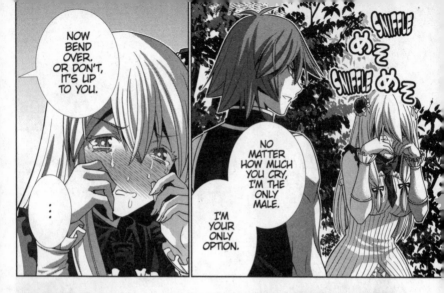

NOW BEND OVER. OR DON'T, IT'S UP TO YOU.

...

SNIFFLE めそ SNIFFLE めそ めそ

NO MATTER HOW MUCH YOU CRY, I'M THE ONLY MALE.

I'M YOUR ONLY OPTION.

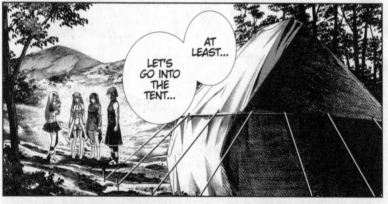

AT LEAST...

LET'S GO INTO THE TENT...

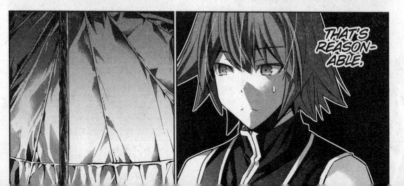

THAT'S REASON-ABLE.

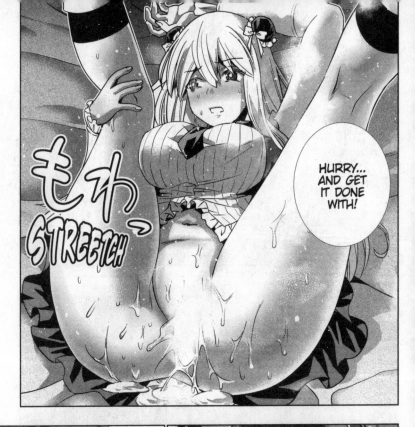

HURRY... AND GET IT DONE WITH!

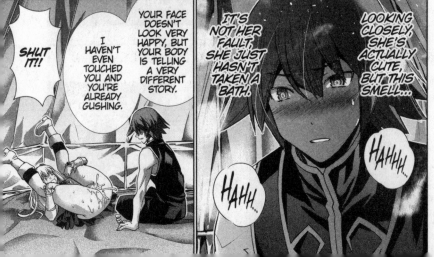

YOUR FACE DOESN'T LOOK VERY HAPPY, BUT YOUR BODY IS TELLING A VERY DIFFERENT STORY.

I HAVEN'T EVEN TOUCHED YOU AND YOU'RE ALREADY GUSHING.

SHUT IT!!

IT'S NOT HER FAULT, SHE JUST HASN'T TAKEN A BATH.

LOOKING CLOSELY, SHE'S ACTUALLY CUTE, BUT THIS SMELL...

HAHHH...

HAHH...

HAHH...

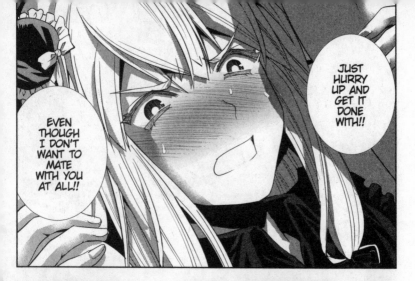

JUST HURRY UP AND GET IT DONE WITH!!

EVEN THOUGH I DON'T WANT TO MATE WITH YOU AT ALL!!

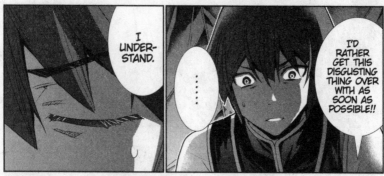

I UNDERSTAND.

......

I'D RATHER GET THIS DISGUSTING THING OVER WITH AS SOON AS POSSIBLE!!

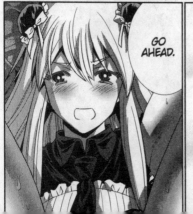

GO AHEAD.

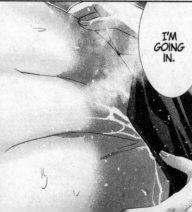

I'M GOING IN.

SHUDDER
AH-HH-HH-HH-HH-!!
SHUDDER
SHUDDER
SHPLURRT!

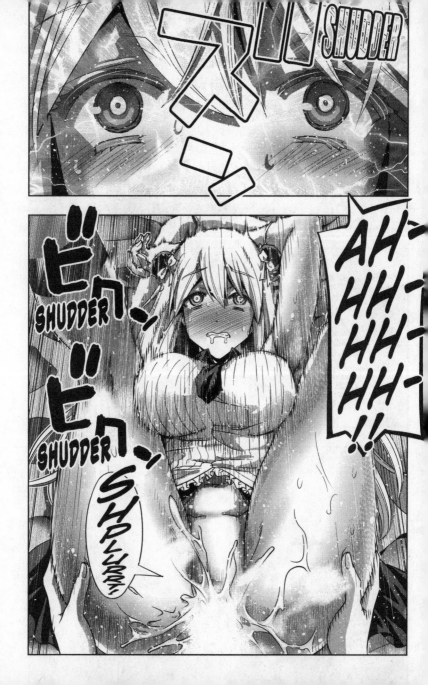

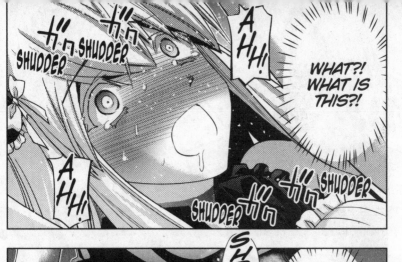

SHUDDER SHUDDER SHUDDER

AHH!

AHH!

WHAT?! WHAT IS THIS?!

SHUDDER SHUDDER

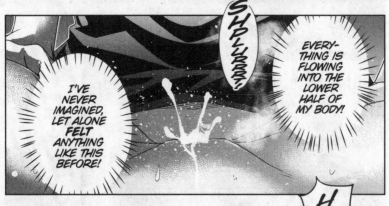

SHPLURRR!

I'VE NEVER IMAGINED, LET ALONE FELT ANYTHING LIKE THIS BEFORE!

EVERYTHING IS FLOWING INTO THE LOWER HALF OF MY BODY!

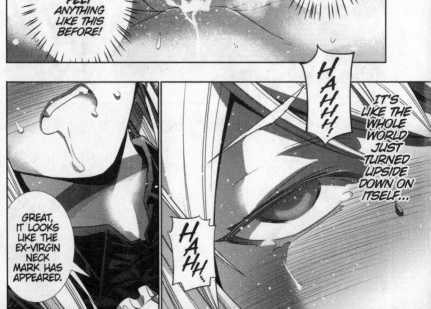

HAHHH!

IT'S LIKE THE WHOLE WORLD JUST TURNED UPSIDE DOWN ON ITSELF...

GREAT, IT LOOKS LIKE THE EX-VIRGIN NECK MARK HAS APPEARED.

HAHH...

THAT SHOULD DO IT THEN.
NOW LET'S GET ON THE BICORN AND HEAD TOWARD SANDRIO.
SHLIIP
?!
BUT...
BUT IF YOU APOLOGIZE FOR HOW RUDE YOU'VE BEEN, MAYBE I'LL KEEP MATING WITH YOU.
HAHHHH!
HAHHHH!
HAHHHH!
HAHHHH!
NOW WHAT WILL YOU DO?
WILL THIS LITTLE BRAT...
GIVE IN?
OR WILL SHE RESIST...?

SOB
ポロ
SOB
ポロ
HUH ?!
HAHHHH!
HAHHHH!
MY HERO-SAMA ...
HERO-SAMA ...
I HUMBLY APOLOGIZE... FOR MY IMPERTINENCE AND SNOBBERY...
I AM NOTHING, BUT I PLEASE ASK THAT YOU CONTINUE MATING WITH ME, PLEASE...
くぱぁ
SPREAAD
YOU DON'T NEED TO GO THAT FAR!!
ビュル
ビュルッ
SHPLURT
SHPLURTT

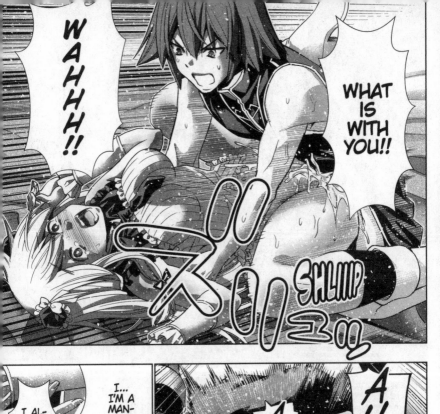

WAHHH!!

WHAT IS WITH YOU!!

SHLIIIP

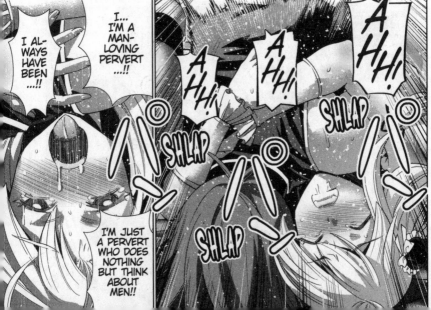

I ALWAYS HAVE BEEN ...!!

I... I'M A MAN-LOVING PERVERT ...!!

AHH!

AHH!

AHH!

SHLAP

SHLAP

SHLAP

I'M JUST A PERVERT WHO DOES NOTHING BUT THINK ABOUT MEN!!

I HAD NO IDEA ...
SQUELCH
AHHHH!
AHH!
SHLAP
SHLAP
SHLAP
MALES WERE SUCH POWERFUL CREATURES ...!!
SHPLURRT
THEY ARE COMPLETELY DIFFERENT ...!!
SHLAP
AHHHH!
FROM FEMALES ...!!
SHPLURT
SHLAP
SHLAP
AHH!

HAHHH!
HAHHH!
HAHHH!
HAHHH!
TUG ちょん ちょん TUG
HAHH!
HAHH!
HAHH!
FUU...
ちゅぱっ SHLURP
FUU...
ちゅぱっ SHLURP

HAHHHH!
ジュルル
SHPLURT
HAHHHH!
ジュル
SHPLURRT
ちゅぱっ
SHLURPP
ビュビュッ
SHPLURT
HAHH!
SHPLURT
ちゅぱっ
SHLURPP
HAHHHH!
FUU...
グジュルルル
SHQUIIISH
FUUU...
ブチュッ
SQUISH
ブチュッ
SQUISH
パンパン
SHLAP
SHLAP
AHHHH!
HAHHHH!
COME...
ブル
SHUDDER
ブル
SHUDDER

THUDD
AHNNNN!!!
SHPLURTTTT
SHPLURRRRR
SHUDDER
SHLURPP
SHPLURRRT
SHUDDER
SHUDDER

SHLAP
パンッ
SHLAP
パンッ
SHLAP
パンッ
SHLAP
パンッ
SHLAP
パンッ
HERO-SAMA!! HERO-SAMA!!
AMAZING!! AMAZING!!
SHLAP
パンッ
SHLAP
パンッ
SHLAP
パンッ
OHH!
OHH!
SHLAP
パンッ
OHH!
HAHH!
UNFAIR ...
THEY ARE STILL GOING...
HAHH!
くちゅ
SHQUISHH
くちゅ
SQUISHH

I'M GOING TO COME AGAIN!!
EVEN THOUGH I'M SUPPOSED TO HATE MALES, I COME AS SOON HE'S INSIDE!!
SHPLURT
SHPLURT
AH-HH-HH!
SHOCK
SHOCK
SHOCK
SHUDDER
KAHH!
PEKO...
SHPLURT
SHUDDER

SHE HAS BEEN COMING NONSTOP...
SHLAP
AHHHH!
SHE HAS BECOME AN ANIMAL, FEELING NOTHING BUT PLEASURE...
SHLAP
SHLAP
AHHHH!
AND SCREAMING LIKE AN ANIMAL AT THE TOP OF HER LUNGS.
SQUISH
SQUISH
AHNNN!!
SHUDDER
I'M COMING!!
SHUDDER
SHUDDER
I'M COMING!!

AA-AA-HH-AA!
SHUDDER
SHAKE
SHUDDER
BA-DUMP
SHPLURRT!
SHPLURRRRT!
SHUDDER
SHUDDER

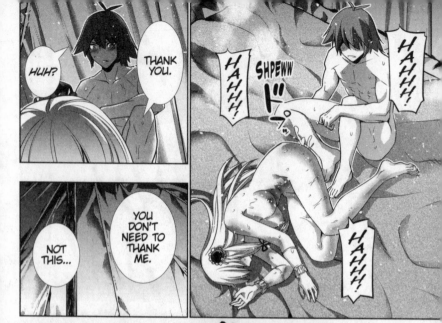

HUH?

THANK YOU.

NOT THIS...

YOU DON'T NEED TO THANK ME.

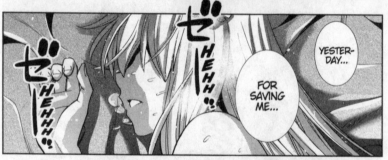

YESTER-DAY...

FOR SAVING ME...

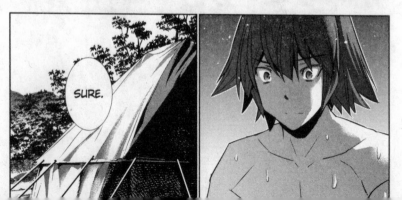

SURE.

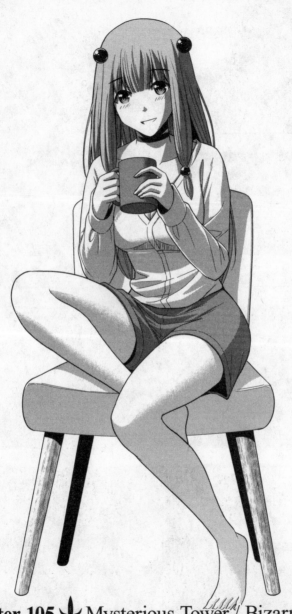

Chapter 105 🌿 Mysterious Tower / Bizarre Forest

CLIPPITY CLOP
タターン
CLIPPITY CLOP
ターン
CLIPPITY CLOP
タターン
CLIPPITY CLOP
タターン
CLIPPITY CLOP
タターン
THIS BICORN HAS NO PROBLEM HOLDING ALL FOUR OF US!
YEAH! IT REALLY IS HUGE!!

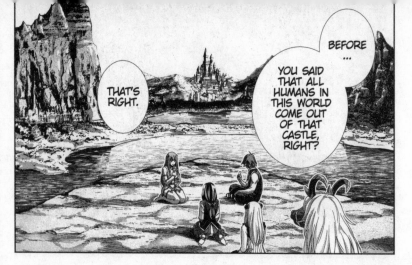

BEFORE...

YOU SAID THAT ALL HUMANS IN THIS WORLD COME OUT OF THAT CASTLE, RIGHT?

THAT'S RIGHT.

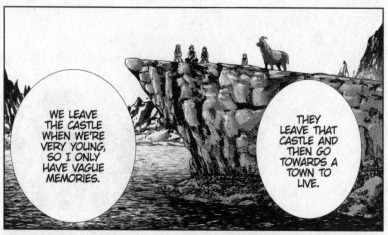

WE LEAVE THE CASTLE WHEN WE'RE VERY YOUNG, SO I ONLY HAVE VAGUE MEMORIES.

THEY LEAVE THAT CASTLE AND THEN GO TOWARDS A TOWN TO LIVE.

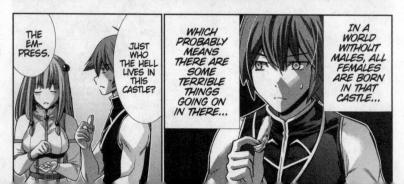

THE EM- PRESS.

JUST WHO THE HELL LIVES IN THIS CASTLE?

WHICH PROBABLY MEANS THERE ARE SOME TERRIBLE THINGS GOING ON IN THERE...

IN A WORLD WITHOUT MALES, ALL FEMALES ARE BORN IN THAT CASTLE...

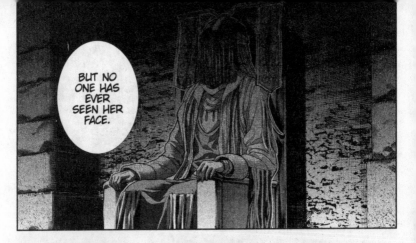

BUT NO ONE HAS EVER SEEN HER FACE.

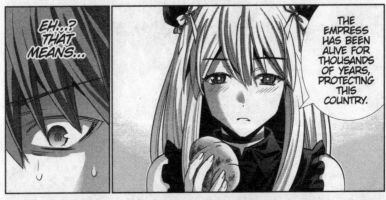

EH...? THAT MEANS...

THE EMPRESS HAS BEEN ALIVE FOR THOUSANDS OF YEARS, PROTECTING THIS COUNTRY.

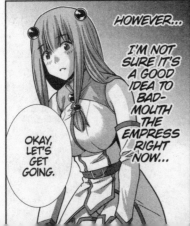

HOWEVER...

I'M NOT SURE IT'S A GOOD IDEA TO BAD-MOUTH THE EMPRESS RIGHT NOW...

OKAY, LET'S GET GOING.

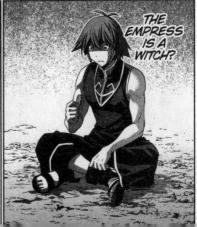

THE EMPRESS IS A WITCH?

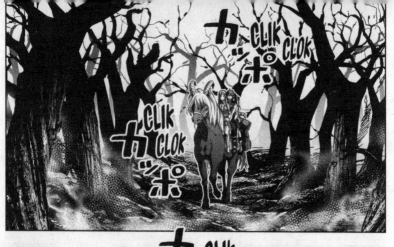

CLIK CLOK
CLIK CLOK

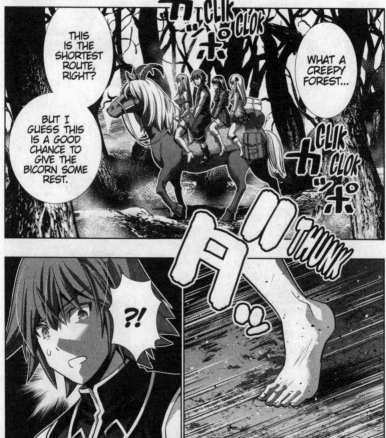

THIS IS THE SHORTEST ROUTE, RIGHT?

BUT I GUESS THIS IS A GOOD CHANCE TO GIVE THE BICORN SOME REST.

WHAT A CREEPY FOREST...

CLIK CLOK

THUNK

?!

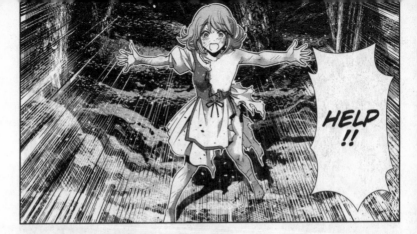

HELP
!!

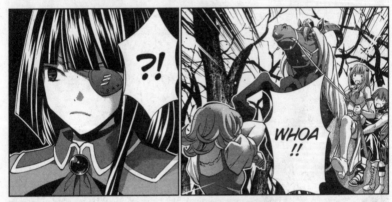

?!

WHOA
!!

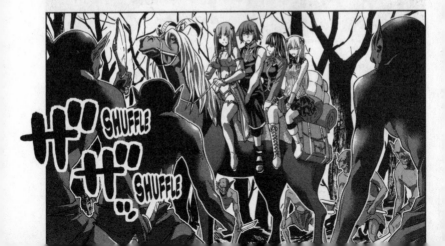

SHUFFLE

SHUFFLE

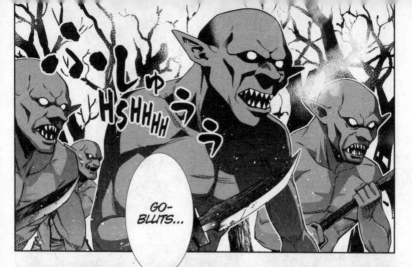

GO-
BLUTS...

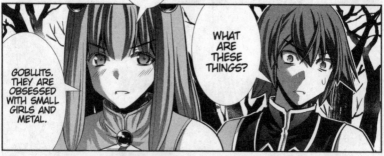

GOBLUTS.
THEY ARE
OBSESSED
WITH SMALL
GIRLS AND
METAL.

WHAT
ARE
THESE
THINGS?

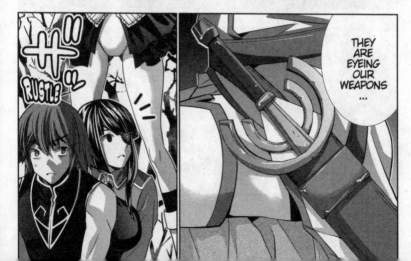

THEY
ARE
EYEING
OUR
WEAPONS
...

PEKO ?!
TRASH...
タ−ッ
WSSK
ズバ
ELAAAASH
バ

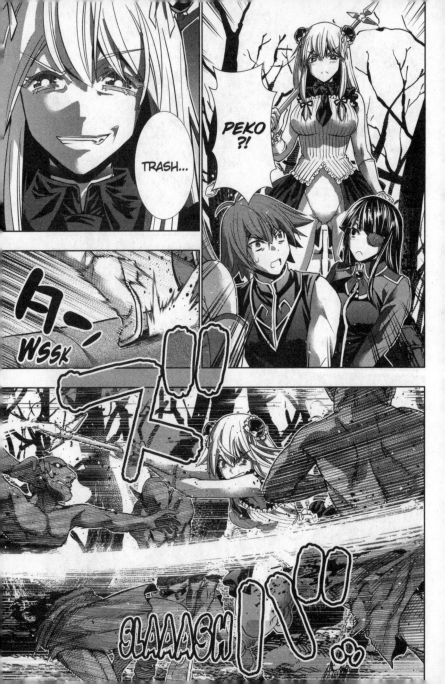

ドサッ THUD
ドサッ THUD
?!
KEKEEE!
KEKEEE!

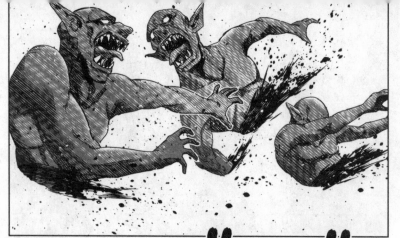

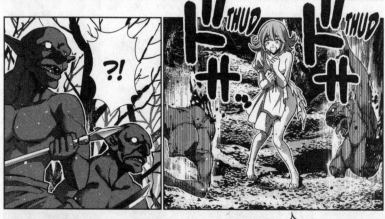

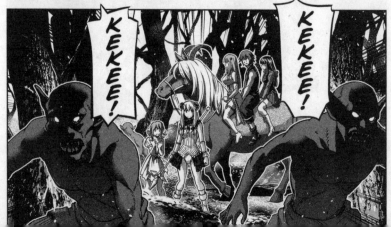

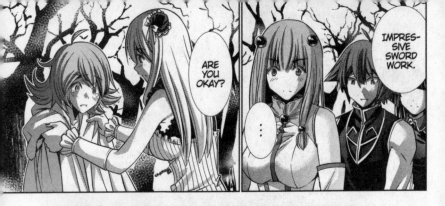

ARE YOU OKAY?

IMPRESSIVE SWORD WORK.

...

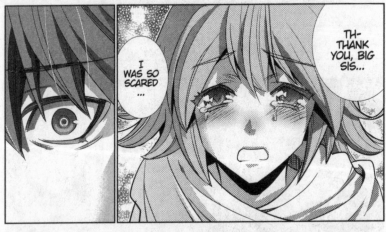

I WAS SO SCARED...

TH- THANK YOU, BIG SIS...

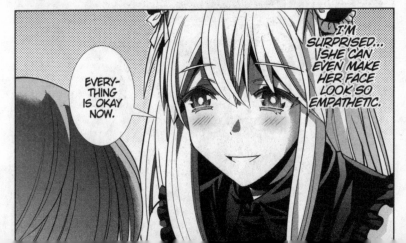

EVERY- THING IS OKAY NOW.

I'M SURPRISED... SHE CAN EVEN MAKE HER FACE LOOK SO EMPATHETIC.

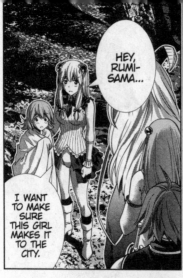

HEY, RUMI-SAMA...

I WANT TO MAKE SURE THIS GIRL MAKES IT TO THE CITY.

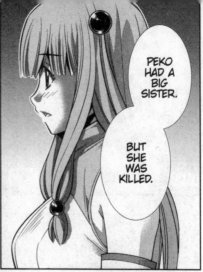

PEKO HAD A BIG SISTER.

BUT SHE WAS KILLED.

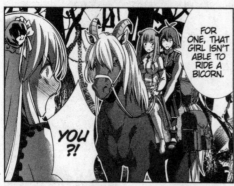

FOR ONE, THAT GIRL ISN'T ABLE TO RIDE A BICORN.

WHY?!

YOU?!

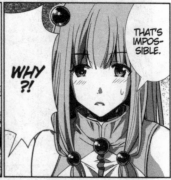

THAT'S IMPOSSIBLE.

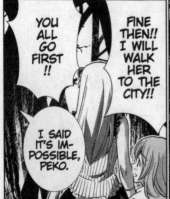

FINE THEN!! I WILL WALK HER TO THE CITY!!

YOU ALL GO FIRST!!

I SAID IT'S IMPOSSIBLE, PEKO.

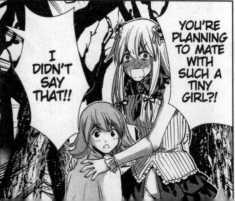

I DIDN'T SAY THAT!!

YOU'RE PLANNING TO MATE WITH SUCH A TINY GIRL?!

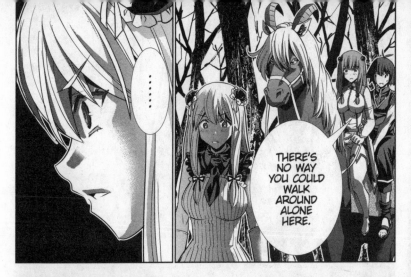

. . . . .

THERE'S NO WAY YOU COULD WALK AROUND ALONE HERE.

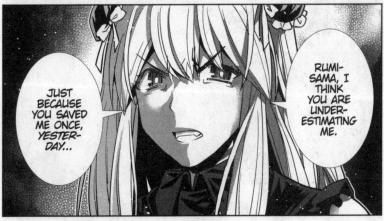

JUST BECAUSE YOU SAVED ME ONCE, YESTER-DAY...

RUMI-SAMA, I THINK YOU ARE UNDER-ESTIMATING ME.

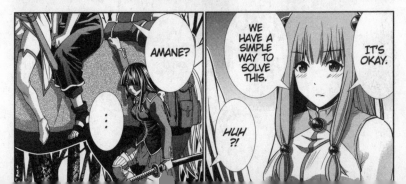

AMANE?

. . .

WE HAVE A SIMPLE WAY TO SOLVE THIS.

IT'S OKAY.

HUH?!

THUNNK
ドッ

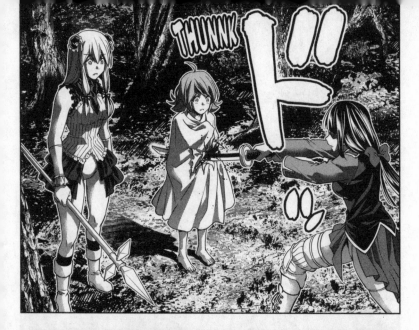

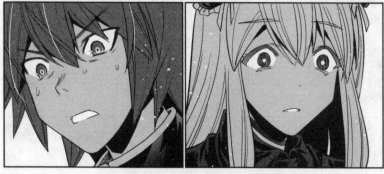

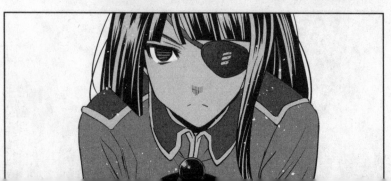

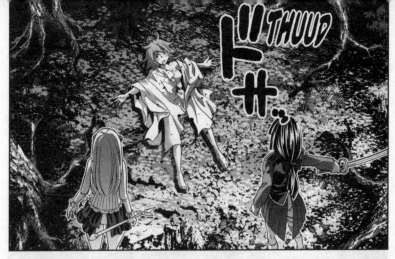

THUUD

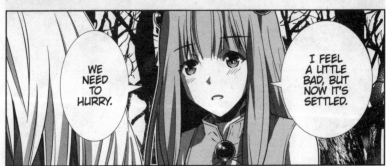

WE NEED TO HURRY.

I FEEL A LITTLE BAD, BUT NOW IT'S SETTLED.

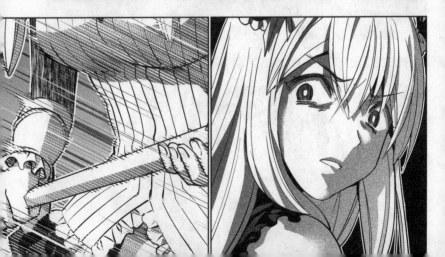

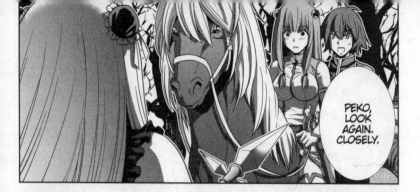

PEKO, LOOK AGAIN. CLOSELY.

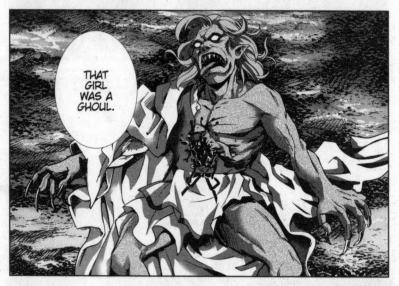

THAT GIRL WAS A GHOUL.

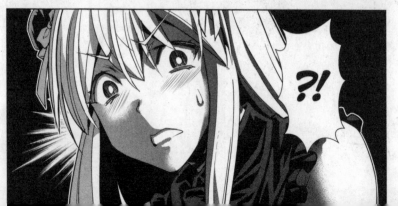

?!

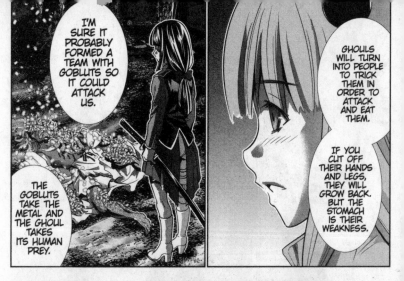

I'M SURE IT PROBABLY FORMED A TEAM WITH GOBLUTS SO IT COULD ATTACK US.

THE GOBLUTS TAKE THE METAL AND THE GHOUL TAKES ITS HUMAN PREY.

GHOULS WILL TURN INTO PEOPLE TO TRICK THEM IN ORDER TO ATTACK AND EAT THEM.

IF YOU CUT OFF THEIR HANDS AND LEGS, THEY WILL GROW BACK. BUT THE STOMACH IS THEIR WEAKNESS.

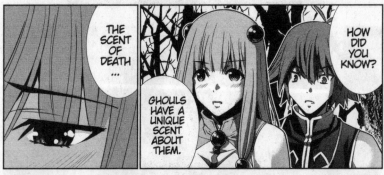

THE SCENT OF DEATH...

GHOULS HAVE A UNIQUE SCENT ABOUT THEM.

HOW DID YOU KNOW?

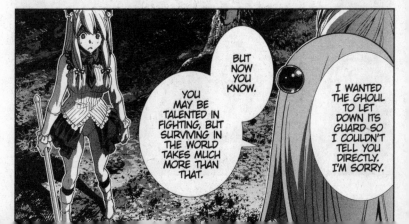

YOU MAY BE TALENTED IN FIGHTING, BUT SURVIVING IN THE WORLD TAKES MUCH MORE THAN THAT.

BUT NOW YOU KNOW.

I WANTED THE GHOUL TO LET DOWN ITS GUARD SO I COULDN'T TELL YOU DIRECTLY. I'M SORRY.

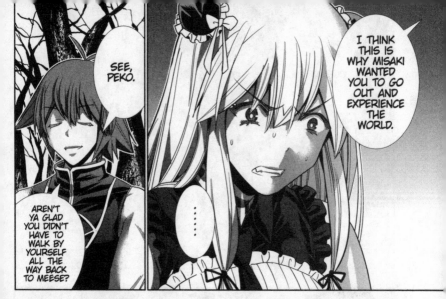

SEE, PEKO.

I THINK THIS IS WHY MISAKI WANTED YOU TO GO OUT AND EXPERIENCE THE WORLD.

AREN'T YA GLAD YOU DIDN'T HAVE TO WALK BY YOURSELF ALL THE WAY BACK TO MEESE?

......

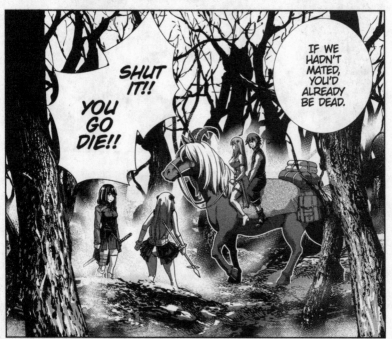

IF WE HADN'T MATED, YOU'D ALREADY BE DEAD.

SHUT IT!!
YOU GO DIE!!

Chapter 106 ✤ Early Army

パカラッ
CLIPPITY
パカラッ
CLOP
ウィーン
WREEEN
ウィーン
WREEEN
ウィーン
WREEEN
パカラッ
CLIPPITY
パカラーッ
CLOP

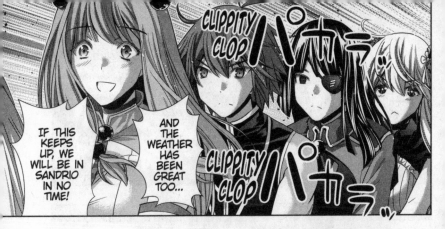

CLIPPITY CLOP パカ

CLIPPITY CLOP パカ

IF THIS KEEPS UP, WE WILL BE IN SANDRIO IN NO TIME!

AND THE WEATHER HAS BEEN GREAT TOO...

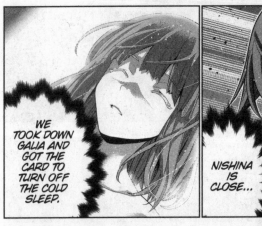

WE TOOK DOWN GALIA AND GOT THE CARD TO TURN OFF THE COLD SLEEP.

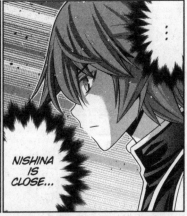

NISHINA IS CLOSE...

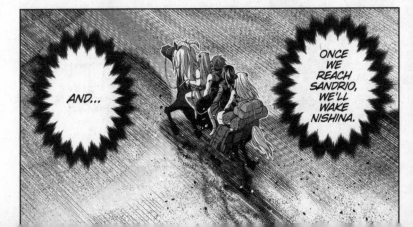

AND...

ONCE WE REACH SANDRIO, WE'LL WAKE NISHINA.

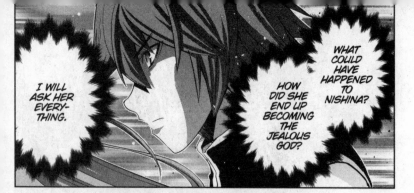

I WILL ASK HER EVERY- THING.

HOW DID SHE END UP BECOMING THE JEALOUS GOD?

WHAT COULD HAVE HAPPENED TO NISHINA?

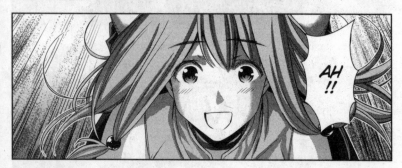

AH !!

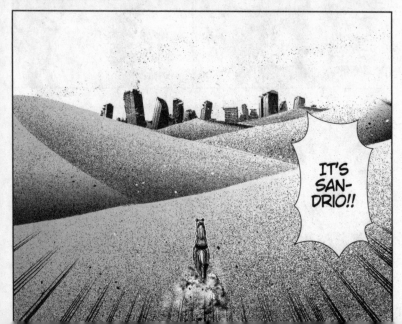

IT'S SAN- DRIO!!

?!
TUG
HUH ?!
WHOOM
NEHHHH!
WHAT'S WRONG, AMANE ?!
WAH!!
WSHH

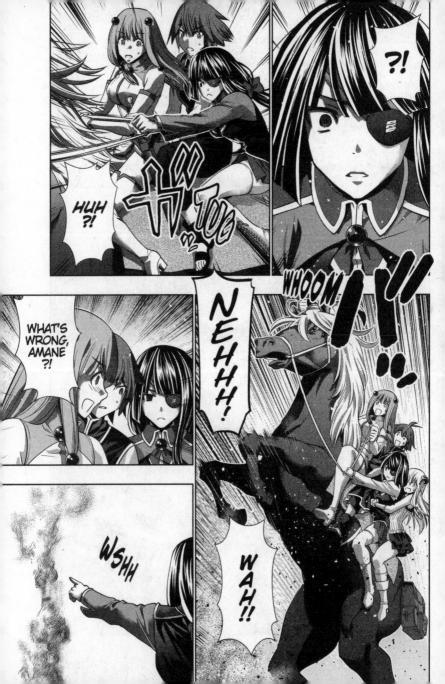

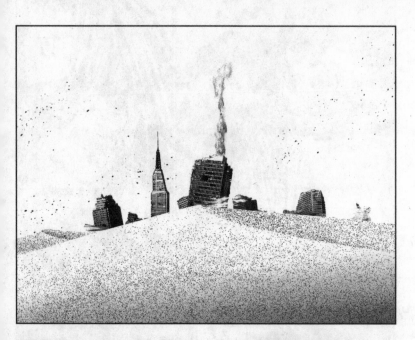

IT'S A BEACON.

WHAT...? IS SOMETHING *BURNING*?

NO.

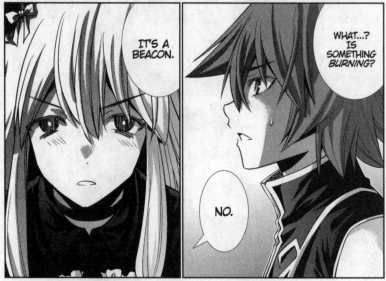

104

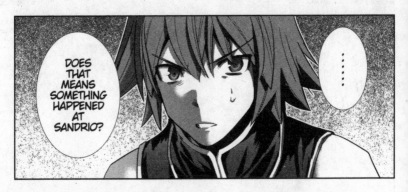

DOES THAT MEANS SOMETHING HAPPENED AT SANDRIO?

. . . .

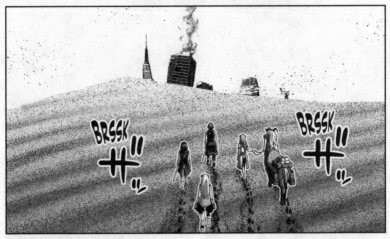

BRSSK !!

BRSSK !!

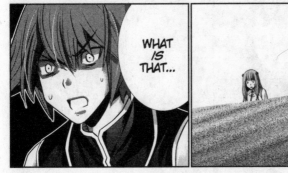

WHAT IS THAT...

BSHHH
NEHEHH

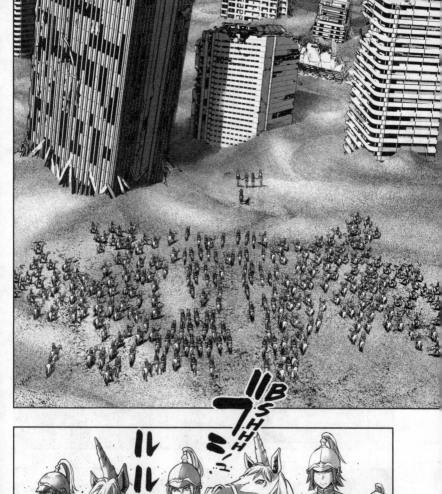

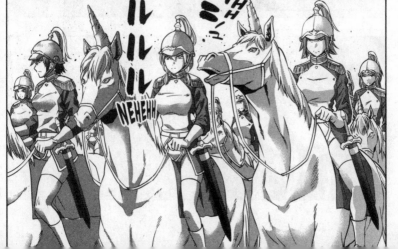

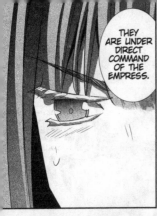

THEY ARE UNDER DIRECT COMMAND OF THE EMPRESS.

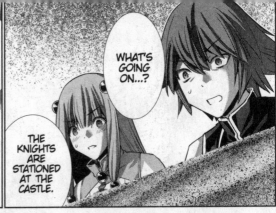

WHAT'S GOING ON...?

THE KNIGHTS ARE STATIONED AT THE CASTLE.

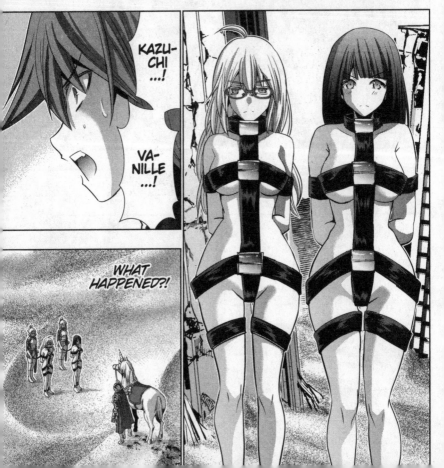

KAZU-CHI...!

VA-NILLE...!

WHAT HAPPENED?!

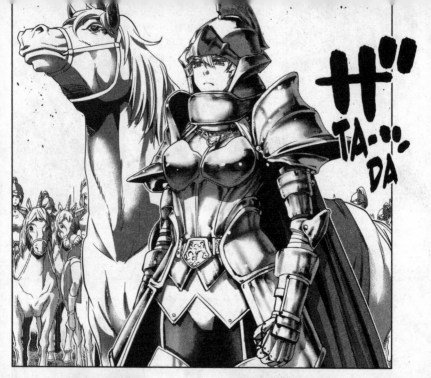

H'' TA-'', DA

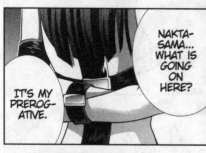

NAKTA-SAMA... WHAT IS GOING ON HERE?

IT'S MY PREROG-ATIVE.

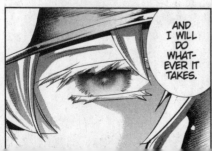

AND I WILL DO WHAT-EVER IT TAKES.

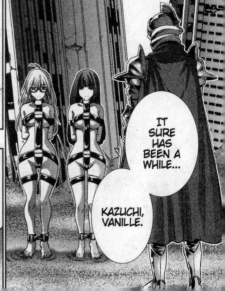

IT SURE HAS BEEN A WHILE...

KAZUCHI, VANILLE.

WHERE IS THE MALE?
YOU WILL TELL ME EVERYTHING.
WE ALREADY KNOW THE MALE IS HERE.
I DON'T KNOW.
ギチ CLENCH
ギチ CLENCH
ギチ CLENCH

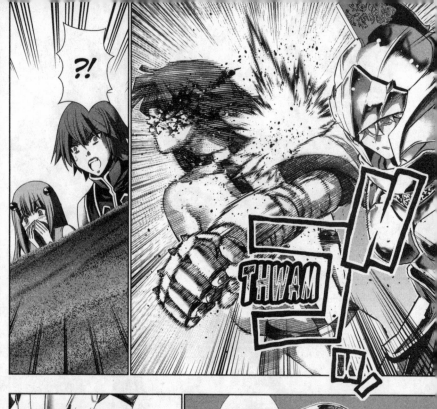

?!

THWAM

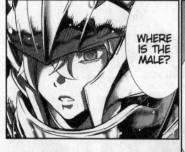

WHERE IS THE MALE?

DO NOT MAKE ME ASK TWICE.

WE'VE ALREADY HEARD ABOUT THE MALE FROM THE EMPRESS.

WHAT ARE THEY TALKING ABOUT?!

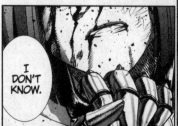

I DON'T KNOW.

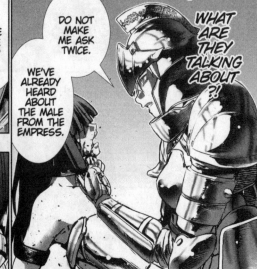

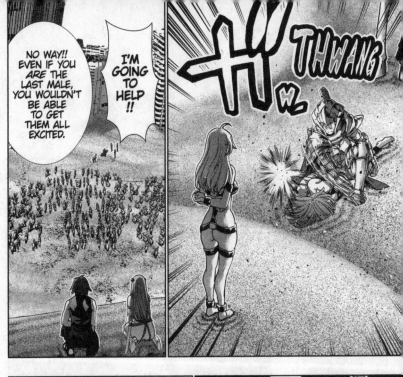

NO WAY!! EVEN IF YOU ARE THE LAST MALE, YOU WOULDN'T BE ABLE TO GET THEM ALL EXCITED.

I'M GOING TO HELP!!

THWANG

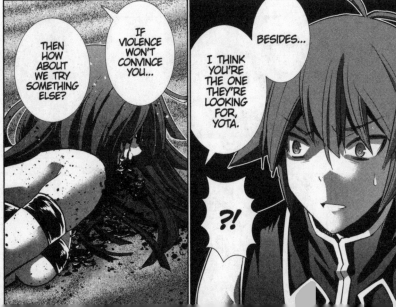

THEN HOW ABOUT WE TRY SOMETHING ELSE?

IF VIOLENCE WON'T CONVINCE YOU...

BESIDES...

I THINK YOU'RE THE ONE THEY'RE LOOKING FOR, YOTA.

?!

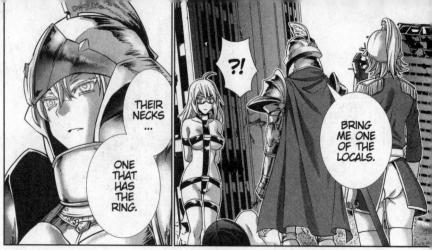

THEIR NECKS ...

ONE THAT HAS THE RING.

?!

BRING ME ONE OF THE LOCALS.

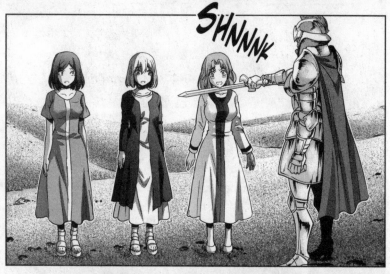

SHNNNK

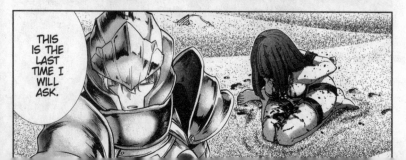

THIS IS THE LAST TIME I WILL ASK.

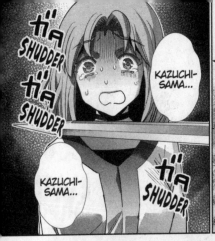

SHUDDER

SHUDDER

KAZUCHI-SAMA...

KAZUCHI-SAMA...

SHUDDER

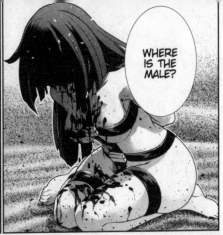

WHERE IS THE MALE?

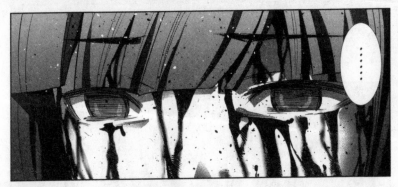

. . . . .

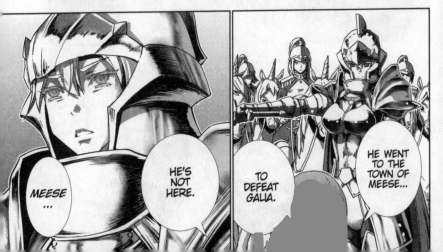

MEESE...

HE'S NOT HERE.

TO DEFEAT GALIA.

HE WENT TO THE TOWN OF MEESE...

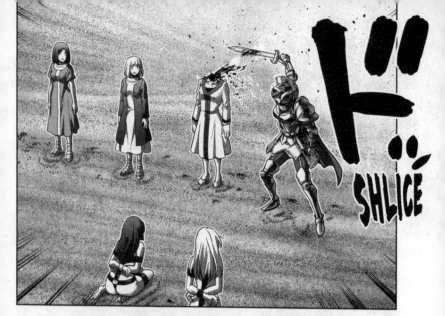

ド...

SHLICE

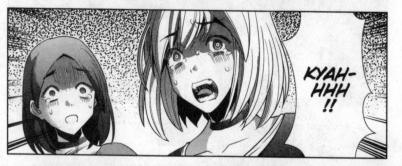

KYAH-
HHH
!!

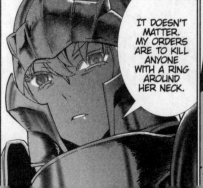

IT DOESN'T
MATTER.
MY ORDERS
ARE TO KILL
ANYONE
WITH A RING
AROUND
HER NECK.

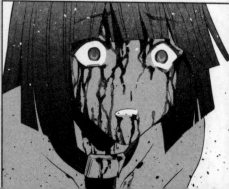

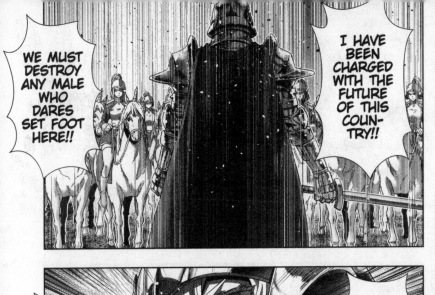

I HAVE BEEN CHARGED WITH THE FUTURE OF THIS COUNTRY!!

WE MUST DESTROY ANY MALE WHO DARES SET FOOT HERE!!

THIS IS THE ORDER FROM THE EMPRESS!!

IF YOU FIND THE MALE, KILL HIM!!

ME RIKU-SA!!

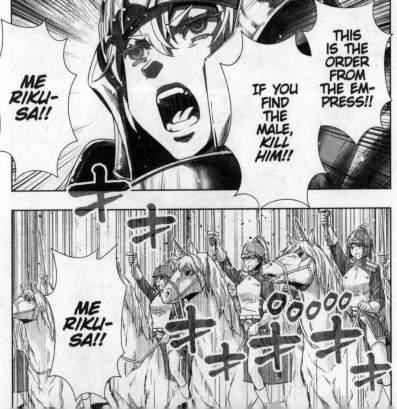

ME RIKU-SA!!

OOOOOO

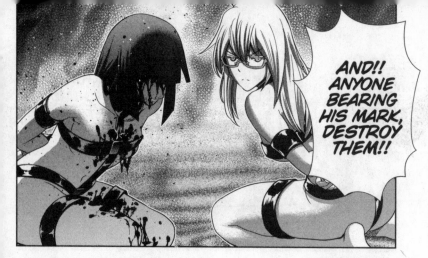

AND!! ANYONE BEARING HIS MARK, DESTROY THEM!!
WHAT...
I WONDER WHAT THEY ARE TALKING ABOUT?
I'M NOT ABLE HEAR WHAT THEY'RE SAYING.
BUT THEY WON'T OUTRIGHT *KILL* ME, NOT THE FIRST MAN IN OVER THREE THOUSAND YEARS.
I WILL GO AND SPEAK WITH THEM.

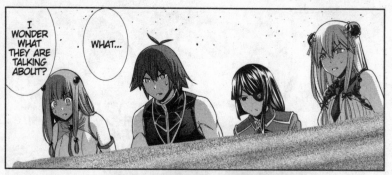

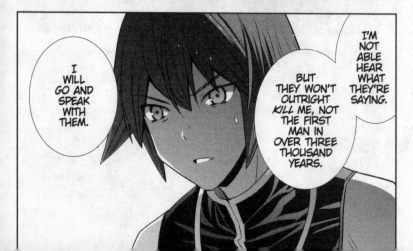

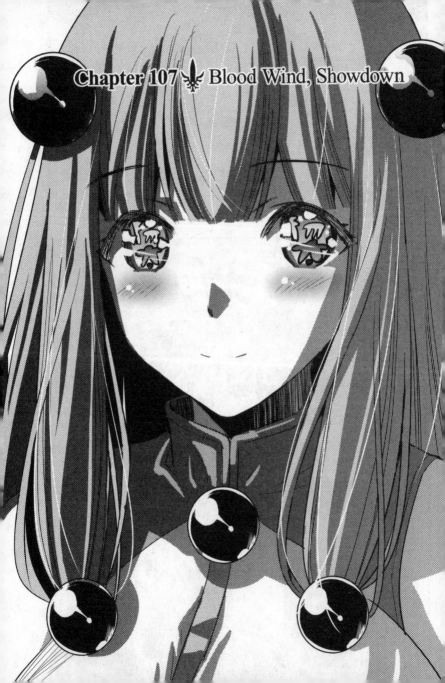

Chapter 107 Blood Wind, Showdown

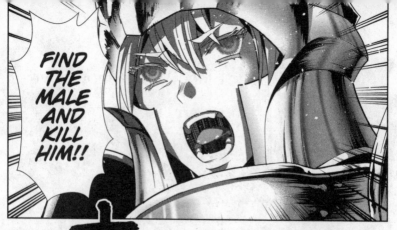

FIND THE MALE AND KILL HIM!!

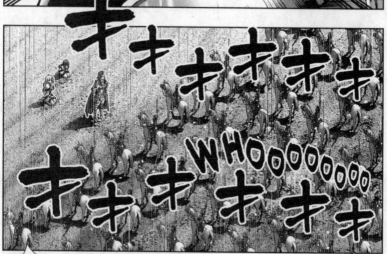

WHOOOOOOOO

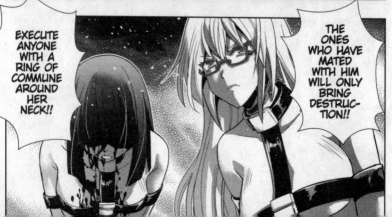

EXECUTE ANYONE WITH A RING OF COMMUNE AROUND HER NECK!!

THE ONES WHO HAVE MATED WITH HIM WILL ONLY BRING DESTRUC-TION!!

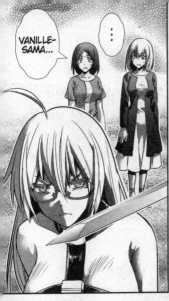

VANILLE-SAMA...

...

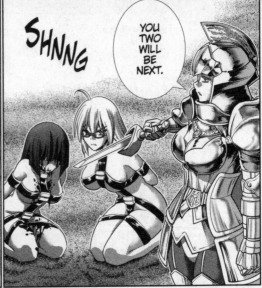

SHNNG

YOU TWO WILL BE NEXT.

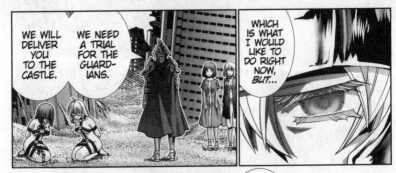

WE WILL DELIVER YOU TO THE CASTLE.

WE NEED A TRIAL FOR THE GUARDIANS.

WHICH IS WHAT I WOULD LIKE TO DO RIGHT NOW, BUT...

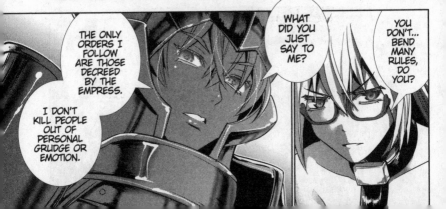

THE ONLY ORDERS I FOLLOW ARE THOSE DECREED BY THE EMPRESS.

I DON'T KILL PEOPLE OUT OF PERSONAL GRUDGE OR EMOTION.

WHAT DID YOU JUST SAY TO ME?

YOU DON'T... BEND MANY RULES, DO YOU?

SHHHHLICE
ドッ
THUD
ドッ
THUD

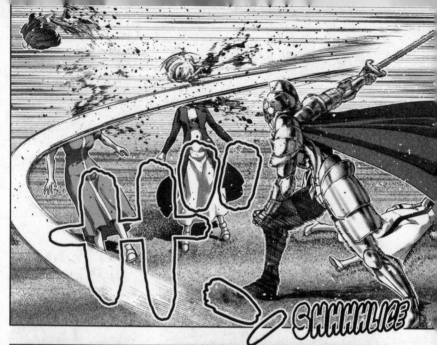

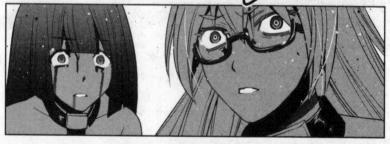

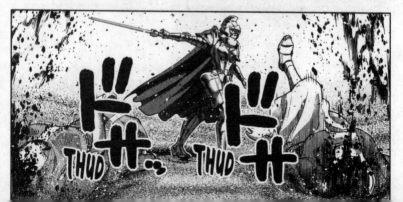

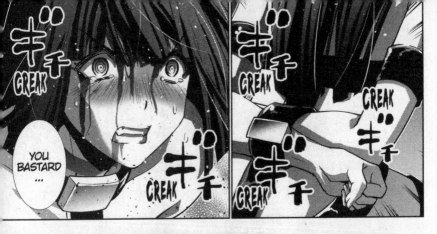

YOU BASTARD...

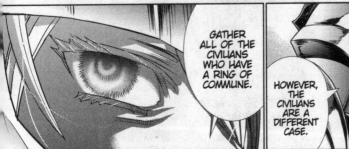

GATHER ALL OF THE CIVILIANS WHO HAVE A RING OF COMMUNE.

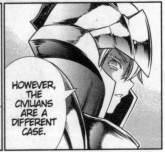

HOWEVER, THE CIVILIANS ARE A DIFFERENT CASE.

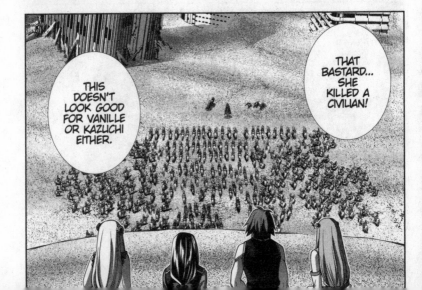

THIS DOESN'T LOOK GOOD FOR VANILLE OR KAZUCHI EITHER.

THAT BASTARD... SHE KILLED A CIVILIAN!

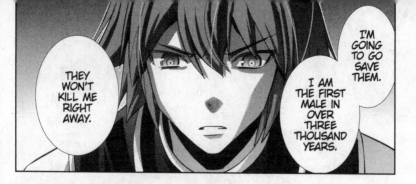

THEY WON'T KILL ME RIGHT AWAY.

I AM THE FIRST MALE IN OVER THREE THOUSAND YEARS.

I'M GOING TO GO SAVE THEM.

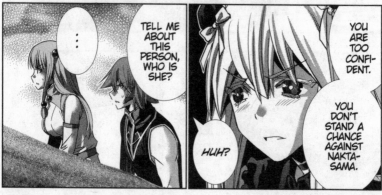

...

TELL ME ABOUT THIS PERSON, WHO IS SHE?

YOU ARE TOO CONFIDENT.

YOU DON'T STAND A CHANCE AGAINST NAKTA-SAMA.

HUH?

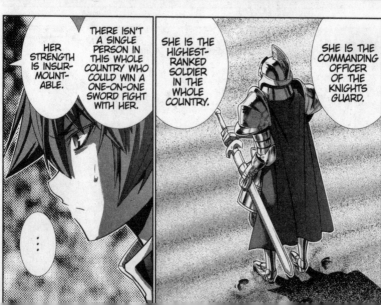

HER STRENGTH IS INSUR-MOUNT-ABLE.

THERE ISN'T A SINGLE PERSON IN THIS WHOLE COUNTRY WHO COULD WIN A ONE-ON-ONE SWORD FIGHT WITH HER.

SHE IS THE HIGHEST-RANKED SOLDIER IN THE WHOLE COUNTRY.

SHE IS THE COMMANDING OFFICER OF THE KNIGHTS GUARD.

...

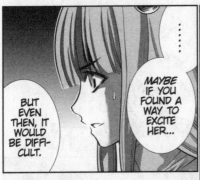

MAYBE IF YOU FOUND A WAY TO EXCITE HER...

BUT EVEN THEN, IT WOULD BE DIFFICULT.

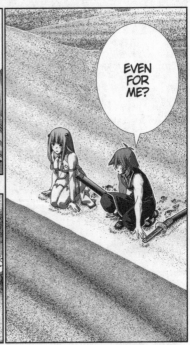

EVEN FOR ME?

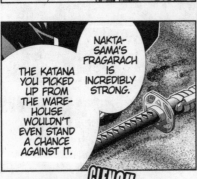

THE KATANA YOU PICKED UP FROM THE WAREHOUSE WOULDN'T EVEN STAND A CHANCE AGAINST IT.

NAKTA-SAMA'S FRAGARACH IS INCREDIBLY STRONG.

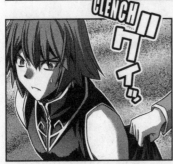

CLENCH

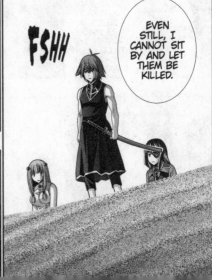

FSHH

EVEN STILL, I CANNOT SIT BY AND LET THEM BE KILLED.

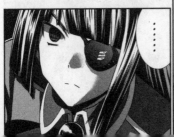

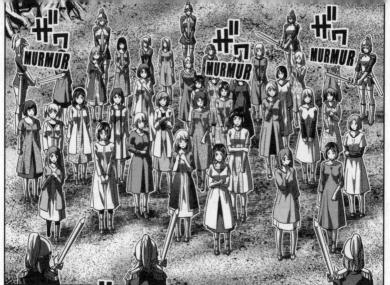

MURMUR MURMUR MURMUR

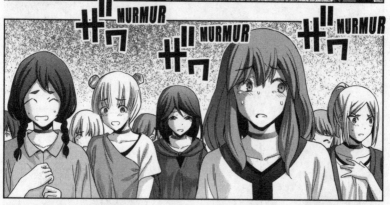

MURMUR MURMUR MURMUR MURMUR

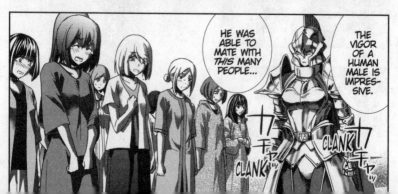

HE WAS ABLE TO MATE WITH *THIS* MANY PEOPLE...

THE VIGOR OF A HUMAN MALE IS IMPRESSIVE.

CLANK CLANK

THE ONES WHO HAVE MATED WITH THE MALE WILL ONLY BRING DESTRUCTION!!
THIS IS AN IRREVOCABLE ORDER FROM THE EMPRESS HERSELF!!
KACHNGG
YOU WILL ALL BE PUT TO DEATH!!
STOP THIS!!
DON'T YOU LAY A FINGER ON THE CIVILIANS!!
NO!!
DO IT.
AH...! AH...!

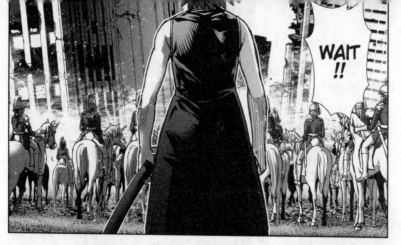

WAIT !!

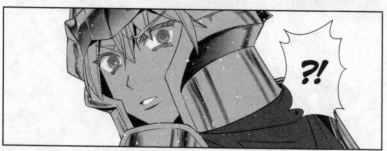

?!

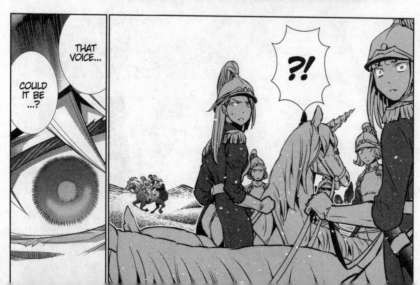

THAT VOICE...

COULD IT BE ...?

?!

THE MALE ?!
GET OUT OF THE WAY!!
FSSH
FSSH
YOU IDIOT ...
DO YOU WANT TO BE KILLED?

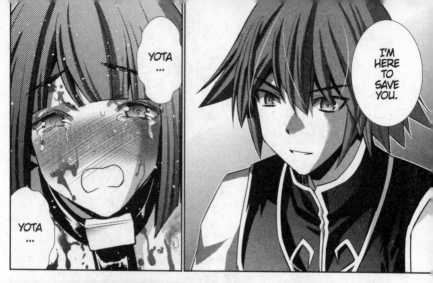

YOTA
...

YOTA
...

I'M HERE TO SAVE YOU.

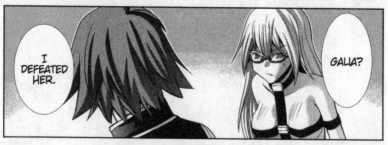

I DEFEATED HER.

GALIA?

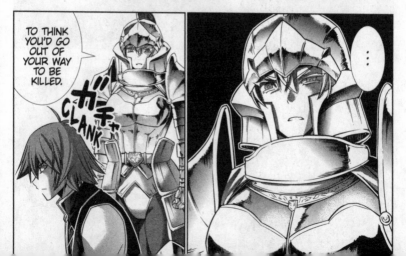

TO THINK YOU'D GO OUT OF YOUR WAY TO BE KILLED.

ガチャ
CLANK

...

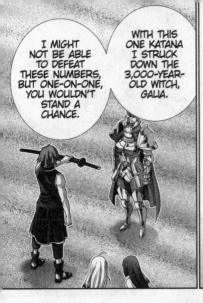

I MIGHT NOT BE ABLE TO DEFEAT THESE NUMBERS, BUT ONE-ON-ONE, YOU WOULDN'T STAND A CHANCE.

WITH THIS ONE KATANA I STRUCK DOWN THE 3,000-YEAR-OLD WITCH, GALIA.

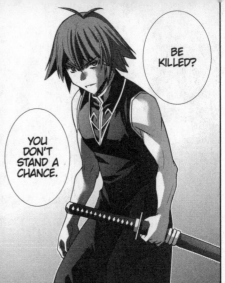

BE KILLED?

YOU DON'T STAND A CHANCE.

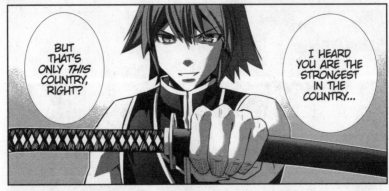

BUT THAT'S ONLY *THIS* COUNTRY, RIGHT?

I HEARD YOU ARE THE STRONGEST IN THE COUNTRY...

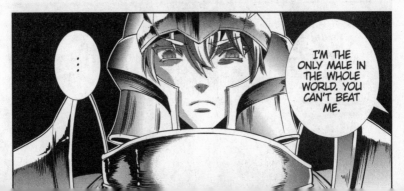

...

I'M THE ONLY MALE IN THE WHOLE WORLD. YOU CAN'T BEAT ME.

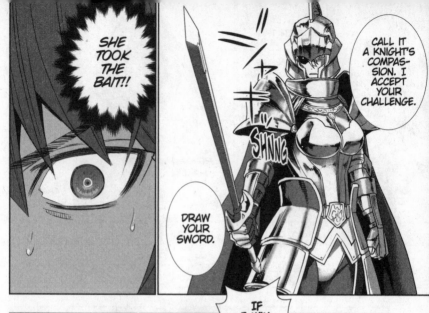

SHE TOOK THE BAIT!!

CALL IT A KNIGHT'S COMPASSION. I ACCEPT YOUR CHALLENGE.

DRAW YOUR SWORD.

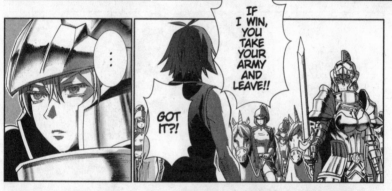

IF I WIN, YOU TAKE YOUR ARMY AND LEAVE!!

GOT IT?!

...

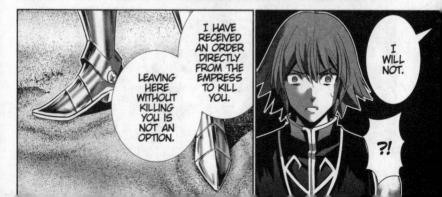

I HAVE RECEIVED AN ORDER DIRECTLY FROM THE EMPRESS TO KILL YOU.

LEAVING HERE WITHOUT KILLING YOU IS NOT AN OPTION.

I WILL NOT.

?!

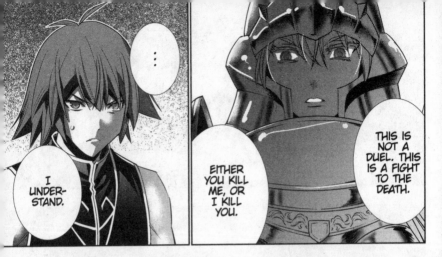

THIS IS NOT A DUEL. THIS IS A FIGHT TO THE DEATH.

EITHER YOU KILL ME, OR I KILL YOU.

:

I UNDERSTAND.

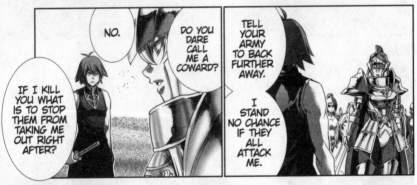

TELL YOUR ARMY TO BACK FURTHER AWAY.

I STAND NO CHANCE IF THEY ALL ATTACK ME.

DO YOU DARE CALL ME A COWARD?

NO.

IF I KILL YOU WHAT IS TO STOP THEM FROM TAKING ME OUT RIGHT AFTER?

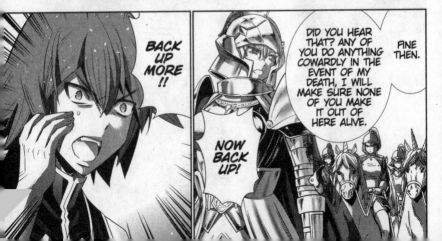

BACK UP MORE!!

NOW BACK UP!

DID YOU HEAR THAT? ANY OF YOU DO ANYTHING COWARDLY IN THE EVENT OF MY DEATH, I WILL MAKE SURE NONE OF YOU MAKE IT OUT OF HERE ALIVE.

FINE THEN.

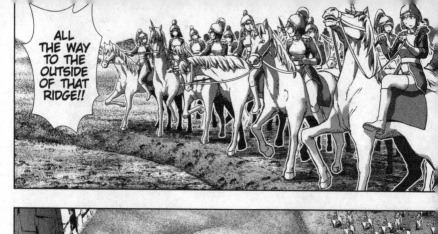

ALL THE WAY TO THE OUTSIDE OF THAT RIDGE!!

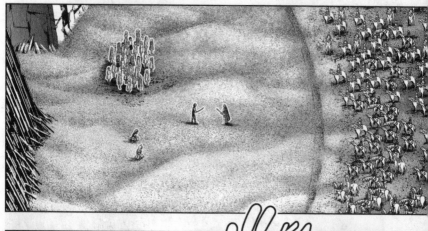

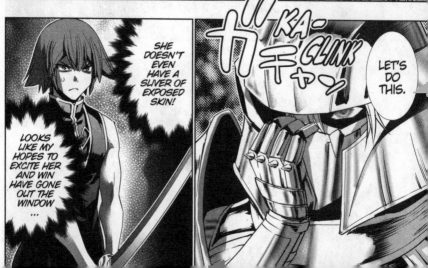

SHE DOESN'T EVEN HAVE A SLIVER OF EXPOSED SKIN!

LOOKS LIKE MY HOPES TO EXCITE HER AND WIN HAVE GONE OUT THE WINDOW...

KA-CLINK

LET'S DO THIS.

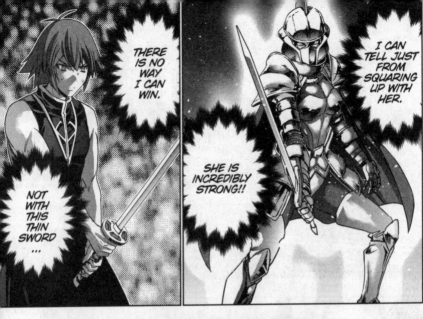

THERE IS NO WAY I CAN WIN.

NOT WITH THIS THIN SWORD ...

I CAN TELL JUST FROM SQUARING UP WITH HER.

SHE IS INCREDIBLY STRONG!!

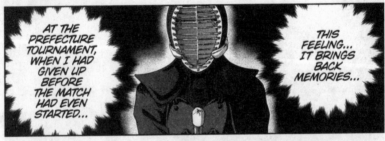

AT THE PREFECTURE TOURNAMENT, WHEN I HAD GIVEN UP BEFORE THE MATCH HAD EVEN STARTED...

THIS FEELING... IT BRINGS BACK MEMORIES...

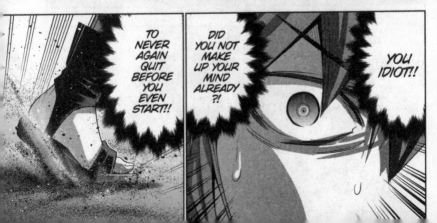

TO NEVER AGAIN QUIT BEFORE YOU EVEN START!!

DID YOU NOT MAKE UP YOUR MIND ALREADY?!

YOU IDIOT!!

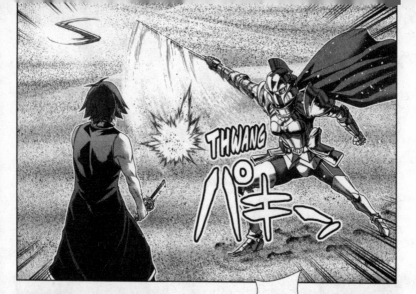

THWANG
パキッ

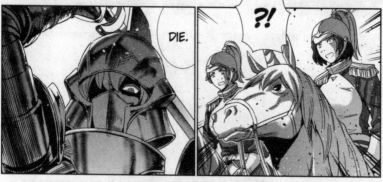

DIE.

?!

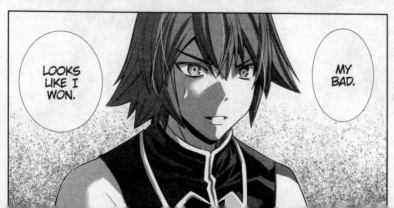

LOOKS
LIKE I
WON.

MY
BAD.

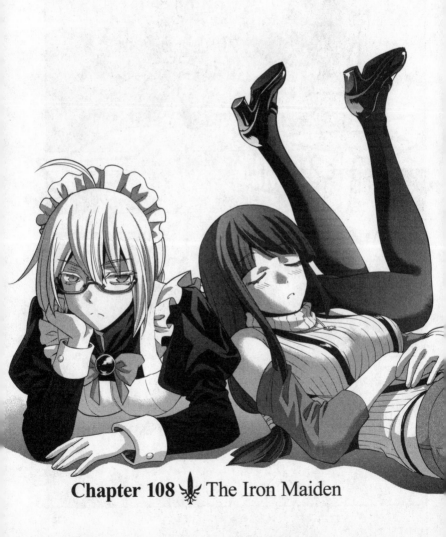

Chapter 108 ✿ The Iron Maiden

THWANG
FSKK
トスッ
?!

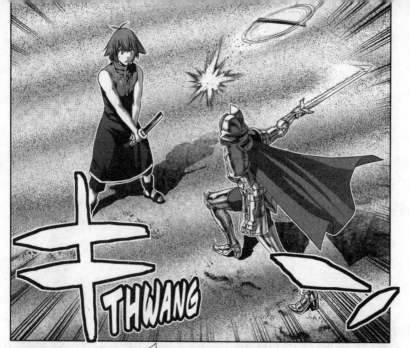

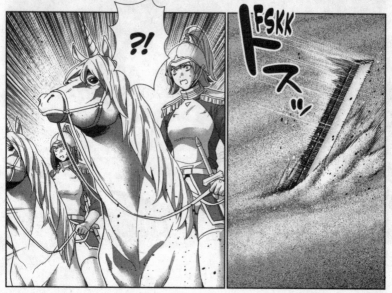

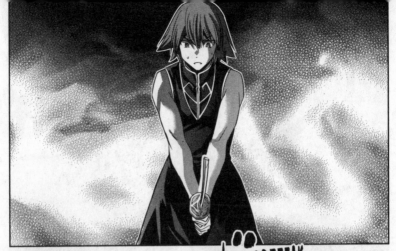

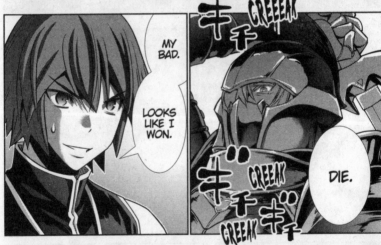

ギチ CREEEAK

MY BAD.

LOOKS LIKE I WON.

ギチ CREEAK

ギチ

CREEAK ギチ

DIE.

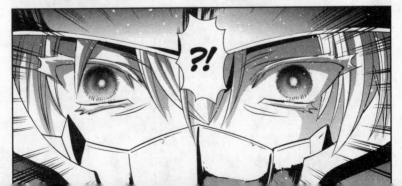

?!

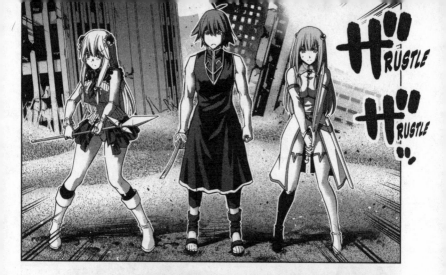

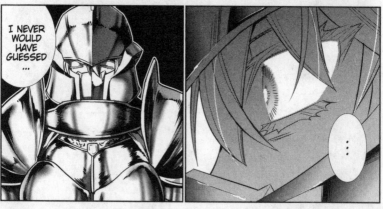

I NEVER WOULD HAVE GUESSED...

...

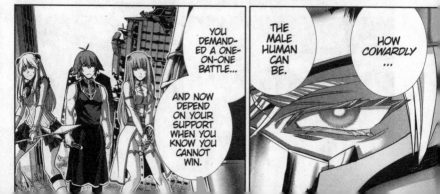

YOU DEMAND-ED A ONE-ON-ONE BATTLE...

AND NOW DEPEND ON YOUR SUPPORT WHEN YOU KNOW YOU CANNOT WIN.

THE MALE HUMAN CAN BE.

HOW COWARDLY...

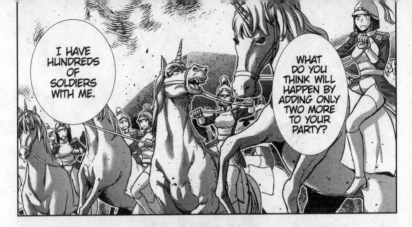

I HAVE HUNDREDS OF SOLDIERS WITH ME.

WHAT DO YOU THINK WILL HAPPEN BY ADDING ONLY TWO MORE TO YOUR PARTY?

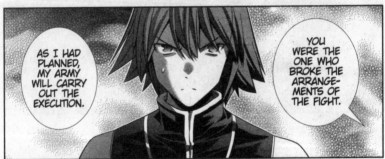

AS I HAD PLANNED, MY ARMY WILL CARRY OUT THE EXECUTION.

YOU WERE THE ONE WHO BROKE THE ARRANGEMENTS OF THE FIGHT.

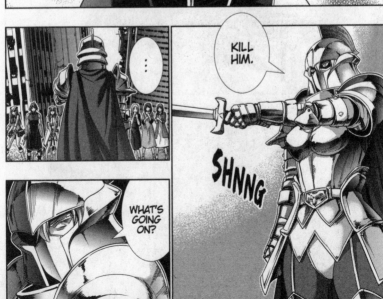

...

KILL HIM.

SHNNG

WHAT'S GOING ON?

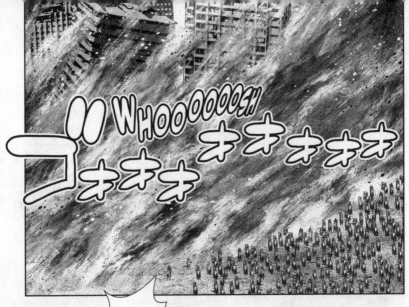

WHOOOOOOSH

NAKTA-SAMA!!

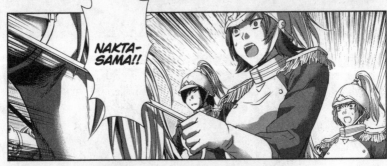

BEEP
BEEP
BEEP

BEEP
BEEP

FOR HUNDREDS OF YEARS, THIS SANDSTORM PROTECTED SANDRIO FROM THE WITCH, GALIA.

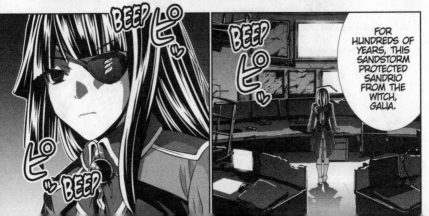

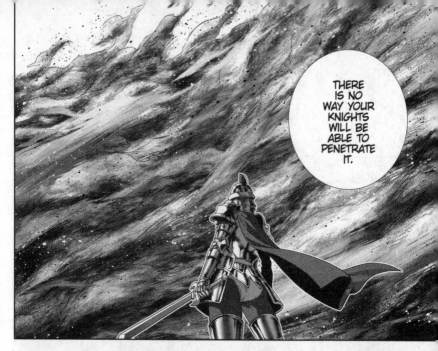

THERE IS NO WAY YOUR KNIGHTS WILL BE ABLE TO PENETRATE IT.

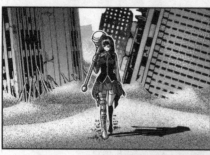

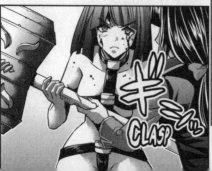

CLASP

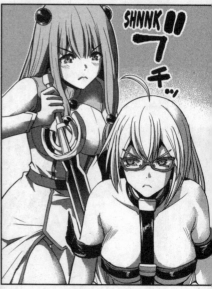

SHNNK

142

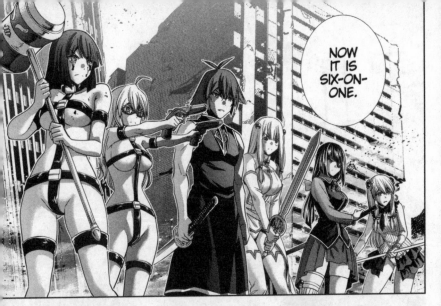

NOW IT IS SIX-ON-ONE.

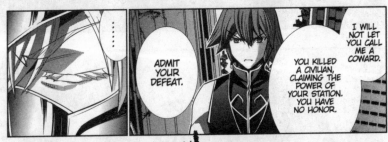

ADMIT YOUR DEFEAT.

YOU KILLED A CIVILIAN, CLAIMING THE POWER OF YOUR STATION. YOU HAVE NO HONOR.

I WILL NOT LET YOU CALL ME A COWARD.

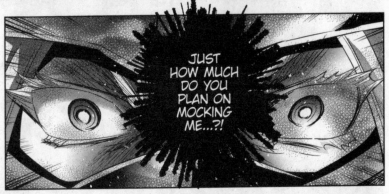

JUST HOW MUCH DO YOU PLAN ON MOCKING ME...?!

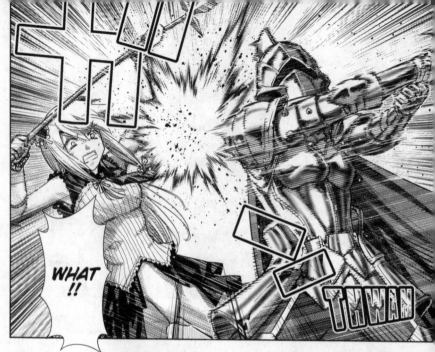

WHAT!!

THWAM

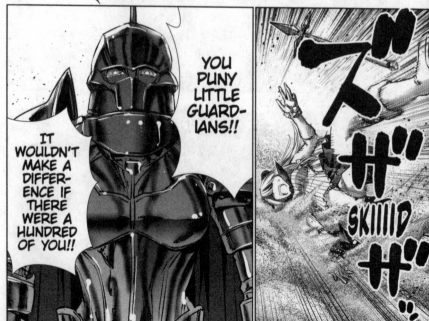

YOU PUNY LITTLE GUARDIANS!!

IT WOULDN'T MAKE A DIFFERENCE IF THERE WERE A HUNDRED OF YOU!!

SKIIIID

TAKE OUT YOUR SWORD !!
HOW DARE YOU KILL THAT INNOCENT GIRL!!
KA-THUD
?!
SHE STOP-PED IT?!

......
YOU'RE A MON-STER...
CREAK
CREAK
CREAK
WHOOM
SKIIIID

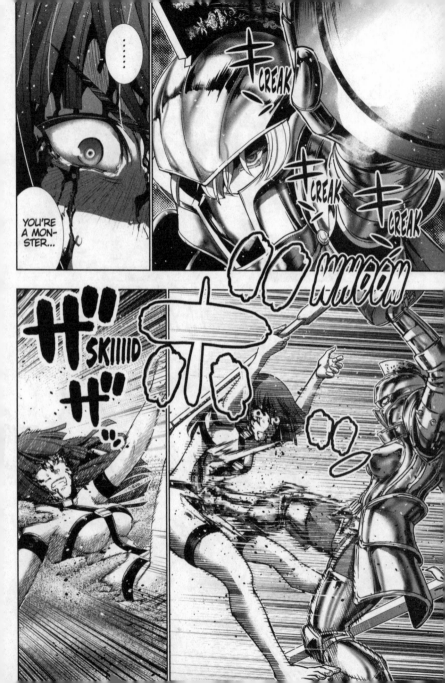

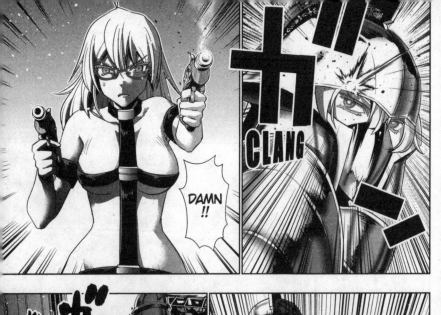

DAMN !!

CLANG

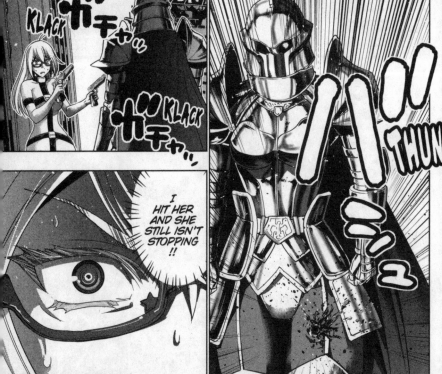

KLACK

KLACK

I HIT HER AND SHE STILL ISN'T STOPPING !!

THUN

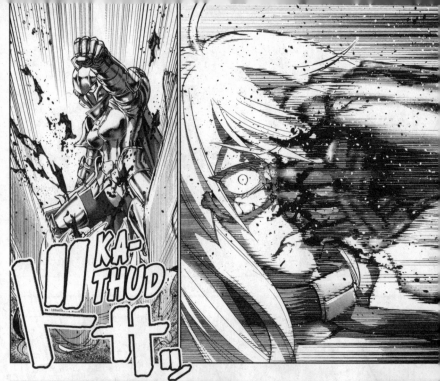

KA-
THUD

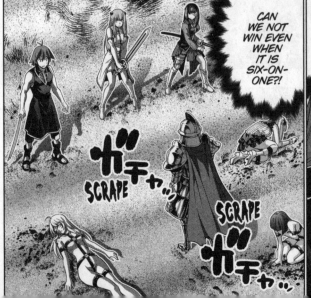

CAN WE NOT WIN EVEN WHEN IT IS SIX-ON-ONE?!

SCRAPE

SCRAPE

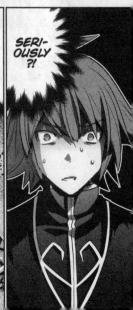

SERI-OUSLY ?!

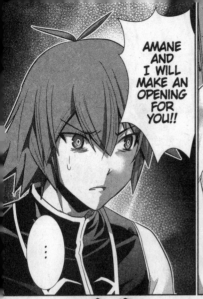

AMANE AND I WILL MAKE AN OPENING FOR YOU!!

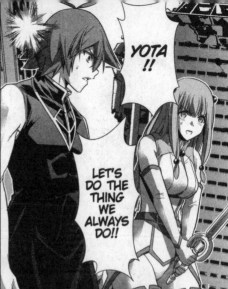

YOTA!!

LET'S DO THE THING WE ALWAYS DO!!

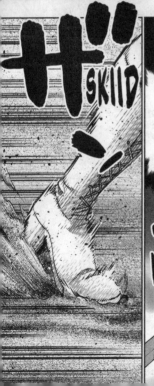

ド SKIIID

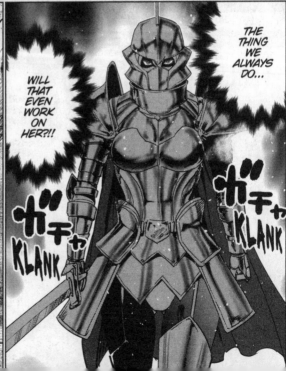

THE THING WE ALWAYS DO...

WILL THAT EVEN WORK ON HER?!!

ガチャ KLANK

ガチャ KLANK

KLAAANG
......
WHERE THE HELL ARE YOU AIMING?
WHOOSH
SHNNK

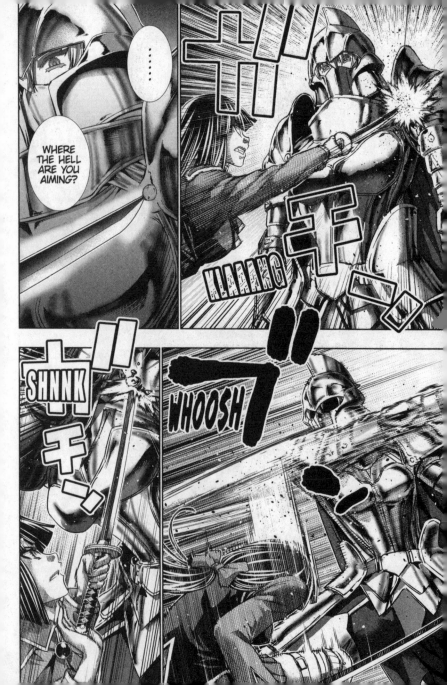

WHAM
KLANNG
THWAM
...
WHAT THE HELL ARE YOU ALL AFTER?!
YOU ANNOYING LITTLE NUI-SANCES !!

CLASP

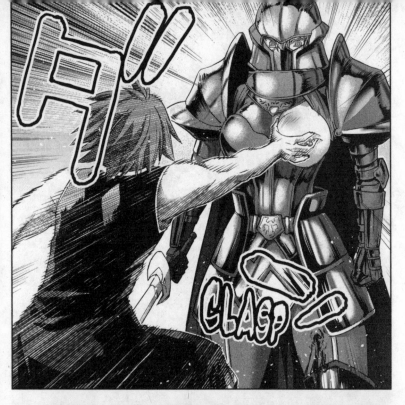

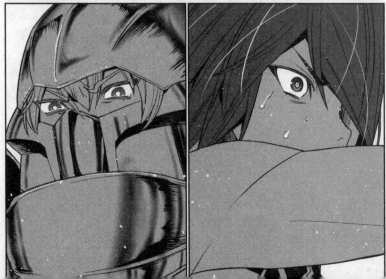

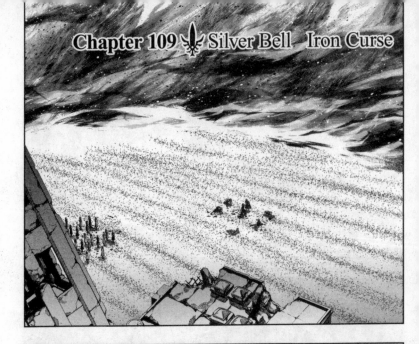

Chapter 109 ✠ Silver Bell Iron Curse

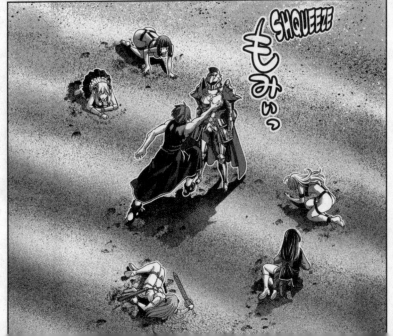

SQUEEZE

もみぃっ

WHOOSH
SKIDDD
WHAA ?!

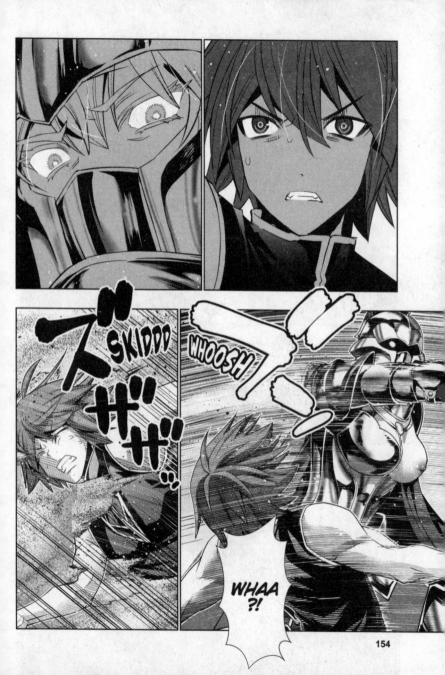

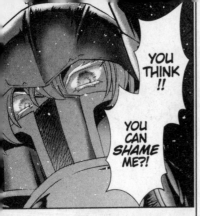

YOU THINK !!

YOU CAN SHAME ME?!

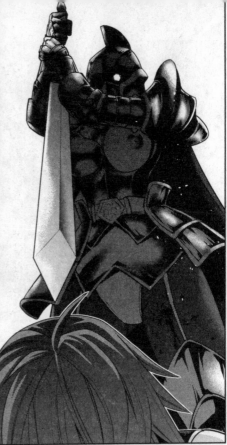

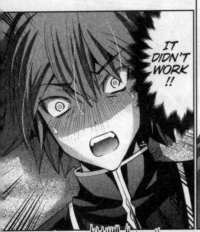

IT DIDN'T WORK !!

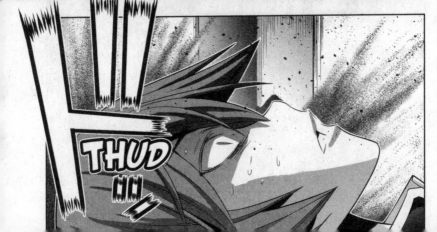

THUD

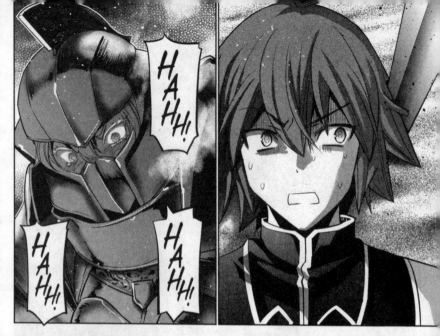

HAHH!

HAHH! HAHH!

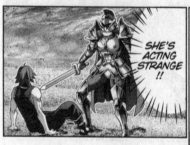

SHE'S ACTING STRANGE !!

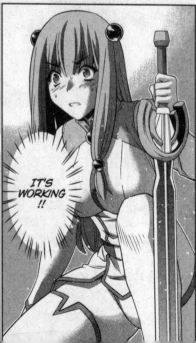

IT'S WORKING !!

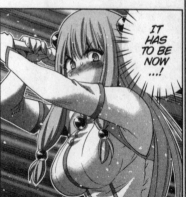

IT HAS TO BE NOW ....!

KLANK
YOTA !!
KSHH

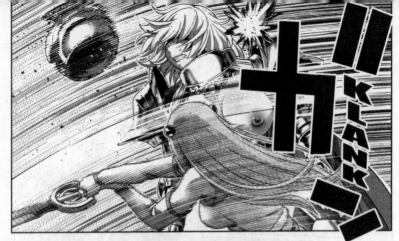

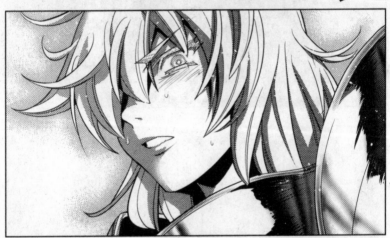

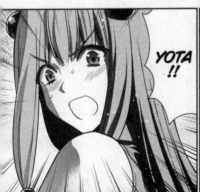

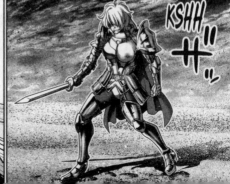

……
SHLURRP
じゅるっ

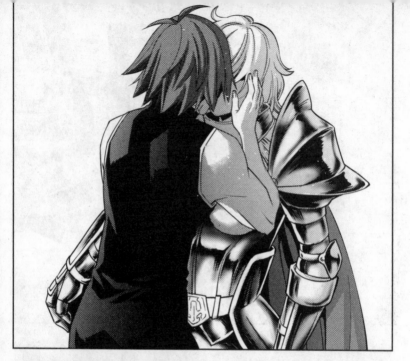

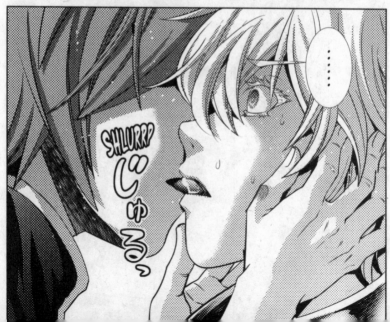

WAIT !!
YOU DON'T NEED TO GO THAT FA--
THWAM
GAHH!!
THUDD
?!

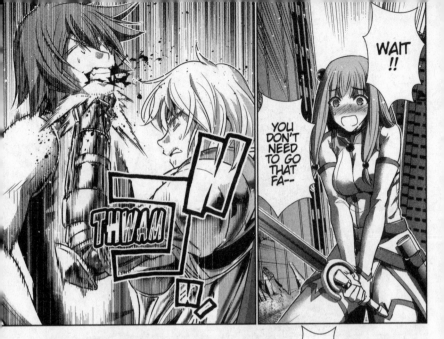

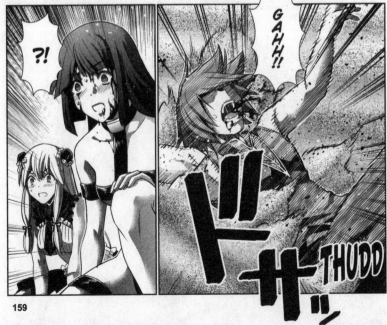

HAHHHH!
HAHHHH!
HAHHHH!
SHPLURT
にゅる
SHPLURT
にゅる
HAHHHH!
YOU...
HAHHHH!
BAS-TARD...
HAHHH!
IT WAS JUST AS THE EMPRESS SAID...
MALES MUST BE KILLED...

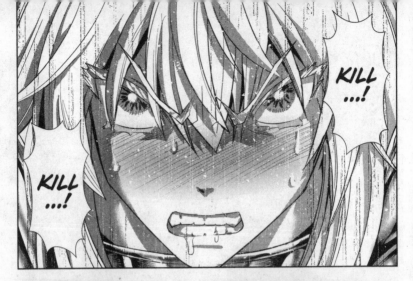

KILL
...!

KILL
...!

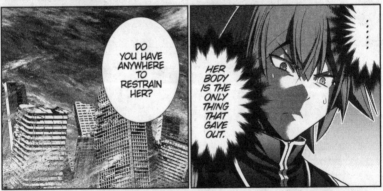

DO YOU HAVE ANYWHERE TO RESTRAIN HER?

HER BODY IS THE ONLY THING THAT GAVE OUT.

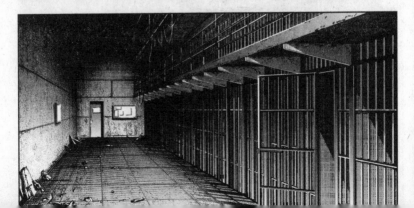

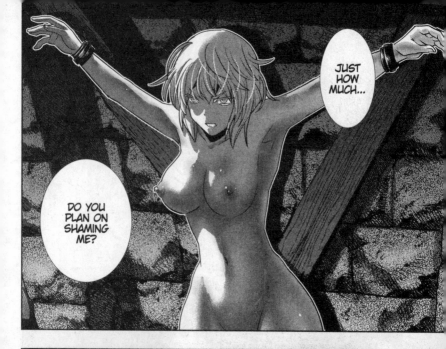

JUST HOW MUCH...

DO YOU PLAN ON SHAMING ME?

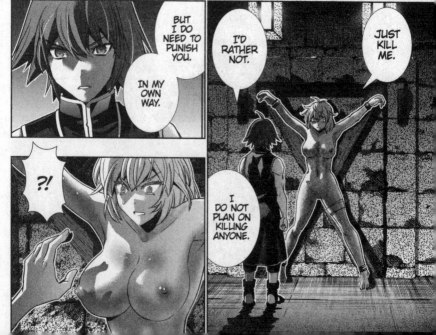

BUT I DO NEED TO PUNISH YOU.

IN MY OWN WAY.

I'D RATHER NOT.

JUST KILL ME.

I DO NOT PLAN ON KILLING ANYONE.

?!

SQUEEEZE
HUH ?!
SHOCK
DRIBBLE
DRIBBLE
YOU BASTARD ...
YOU BASTARD ...
GRIT
GRIT
GRIT
GRIT
GRIT
THE UTTER SHAME ...
KA-CHANK
I'LL KILL YOU ...!!
KA-CHANK
I'LL KILL YOU ...!!

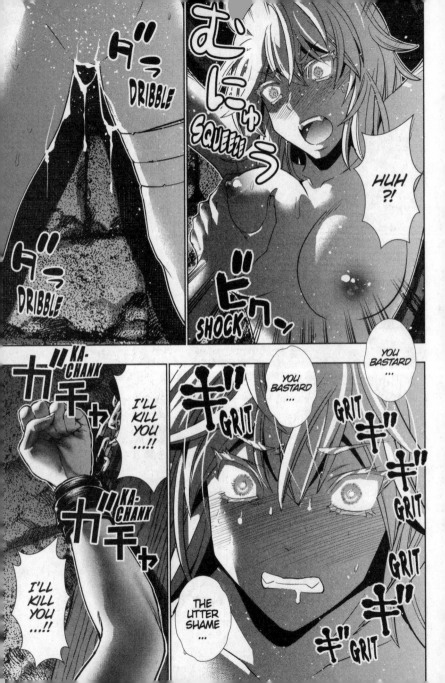

ちゅばっ
SHLURRP
ビクッ
SHUDDER
WAAH ?!
YOU ...
OH? THAT WAS A PRETTY CUTE VOICE JUST NOW.
チュル
SHLURP
チュル
SHLURP
LICK
れろれろ
LICK
ビクッ
SHUDDER
ビクッ
SHUDDER
DAMN YOU ...!
HAHH!
HAHH!
ちゅばっ
SHLURP
ちゅばっ
SHLURP
DAMN YOU...

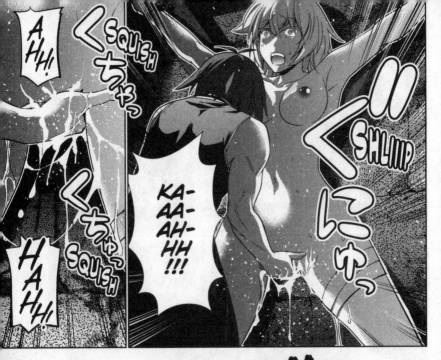

AHH!

SQUISH
くちゃっ

KA-AA-AH-HH!!!

SHLIIIP
くにゃっ

HAHH!

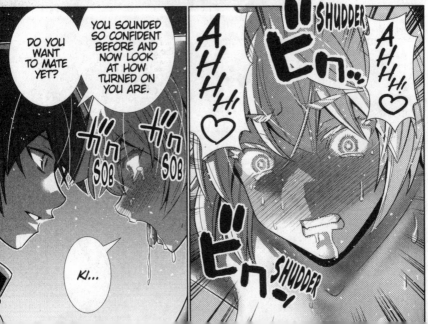

DO YOU WANT TO MATE YET?

YOU SOUNDED SO CONFIDENT BEFORE AND NOW LOOK AT HOW TURNED ON YOU ARE.

SHUDDER
ビク…

AHHH! ♡

AHHH! ♡

ビクッ
SOB

ビクッ
SOB

KI...

ビク…

SHUDDER

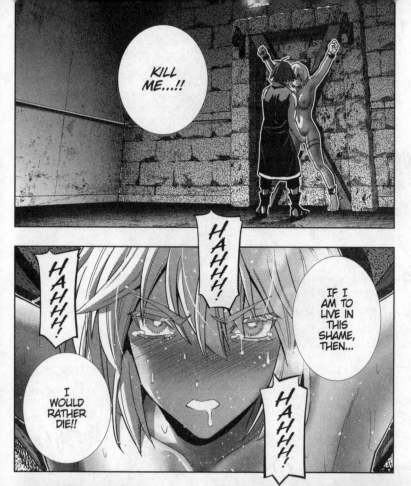

KILL ME...!!

HAHHH!

HAHHH!

HAHHH!

HAHHH!

IF I AM TO LIVE IN THIS SHAME, THEN...

I WOULD RATHER DIE!!

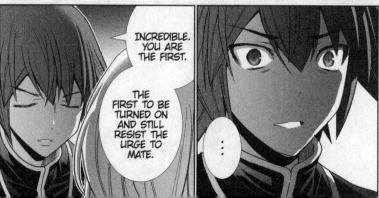

INCREDIBLE. YOU ARE THE FIRST.

THE FIRST TO BE TURNED ON AND STILL RESIST THE URGE TO MATE.

...

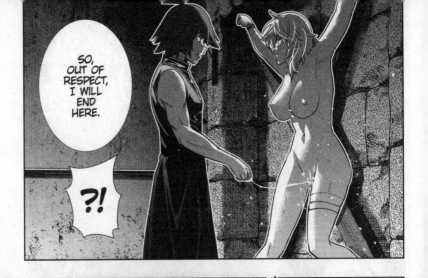

SO, OUT OF RESPECT, I WILL END HERE.

?!

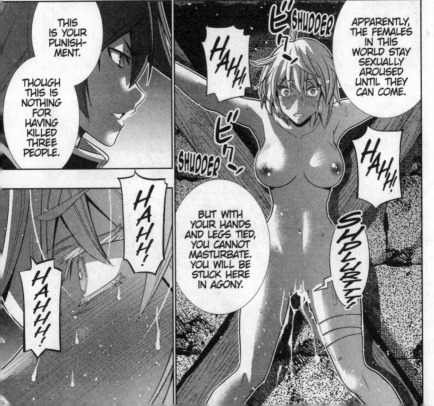

THIS IS YOUR PUNISHMENT.

THOUGH THIS IS NOTHING FOR HAVING KILLED THREE PEOPLE.

HAHH!

HAHHH!

APPARENTLY, THE FEMALES IN THIS WORLD STAY SEXUALLY AROUSED UNTIL THEY CAN COME.

SHUDDER

HAHH!

SHUDDER

HAHH!

SHLURRI!

BUT WITH YOUR HANDS AND LEGS TIED, YOU CANNOT MASTURBATE. YOU WILL BE STUCK HERE IN AGONY.

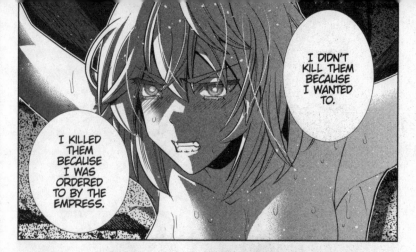

I DIDN'T KILL THEM BECAUSE I WANTED TO.

I KILLED THEM BECAUSE I WAS ORDERED TO BY THE EMPRESS.

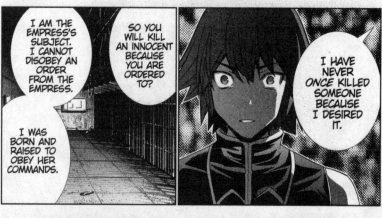

I AM THE EMPRESS'S SUBJECT. I CANNOT DISOBEY AN ORDER FROM THE EMPRESS.

SO YOU WILL KILL AN INNOCENT BECAUSE YOU ARE ORDERED TO?

I WAS BORN AND RAISED TO OBEY HER COMMANDS.

I HAVE NEVER ONCE KILLED SOMEONE BECAUSE I DESIRED IT.

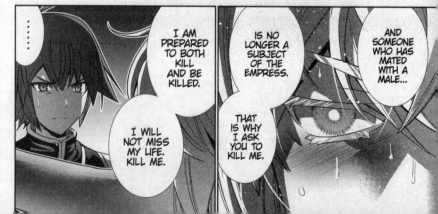

I AM PREPARED TO BOTH KILL AND BE KILLED.

IS NO LONGER A SUBJECT OF THE EMPRESS.

AND SOMEONE WHO HAS MATED WITH A MALE...

I WILL NOT MISS MY LIFE. KILL ME.

THAT IS WHY I ASK YOU TO KILL ME.

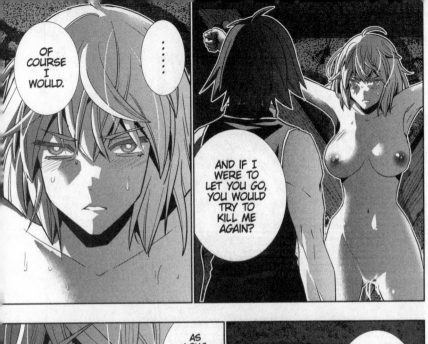

OF COURSE I WOULD.

. . . .

AND IF I WERE TO LET YOU GO, YOU WOULD TRY TO KILL ME AGAIN?

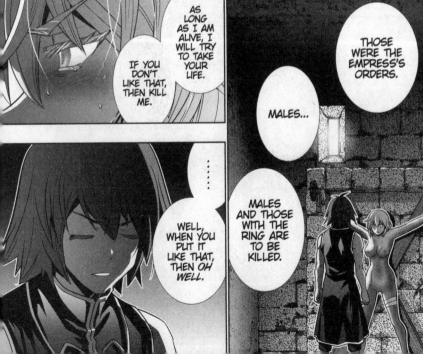

AS LONG AS I AM ALIVE, I WILL TRY TO TAKE YOUR LIFE.

IF YOU DON'T LIKE THAT, THEN KILL ME.

THOSE WERE THE EMPRESS'S ORDERS.

MALES...

. . . .

WELL, WHEN YOU PUT IT LIKE THAT, THEN OH WELL.

MALES AND THOSE WITH THE RING ARE TO BE KILLED.

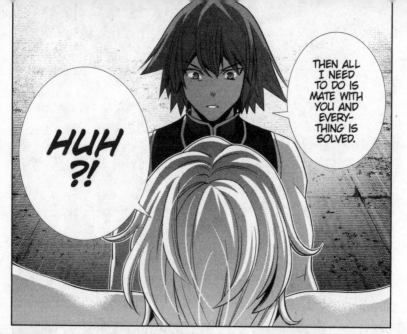

THEN ALL I NEED TO DO IS MATE WITH YOU AND EVERYTHING IS SOLVED.

HUH ?!

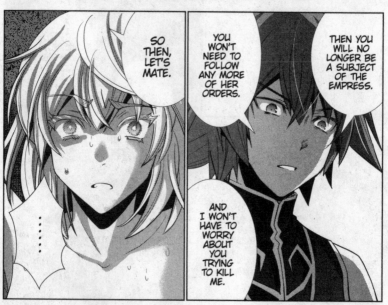

SO THEN, LET'S MATE.

YOU WON'T NEED TO FOLLOW ANY MORE OF HER ORDERS.

THEN YOU WILL NO LONGER BE A SUBJECT OF THE EMPRESS.

AND I WON'T HAVE TO WORRY ABOUT YOU TRYING TO KILL ME.

Chapter 110 White Night

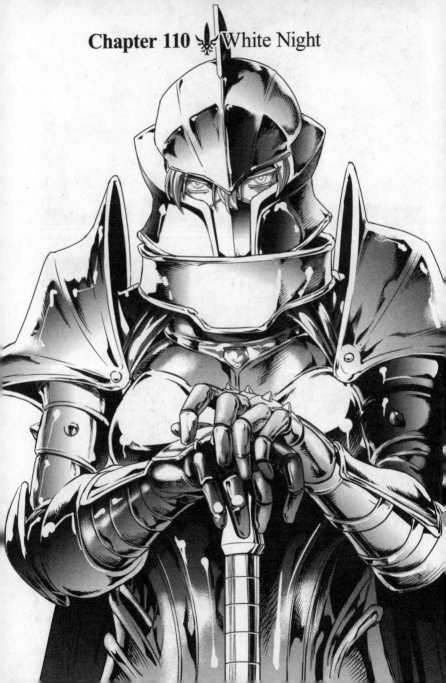

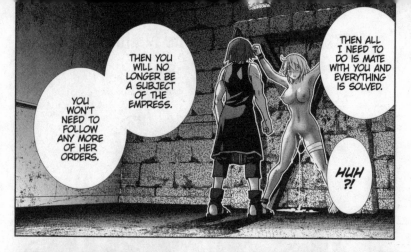

YOU WON'T NEED TO FOLLOW ANY MORE OF HER ORDERS.

THEN YOU WILL NO LONGER BE A SUBJECT OF THE EMPRESS.

THEN ALL I NEED TO DO IS MATE WITH YOU AND EVERYTHING IS SOLVED.

HUH ?!

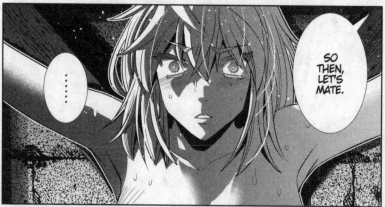

. . . . .

SO THEN, LET'S MATE.

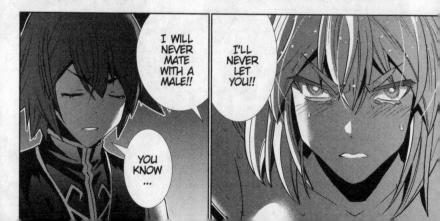

I WILL NEVER MATE WITH A MALE!!

YOU KNOW...

I'LL NEVER LET YOU!!

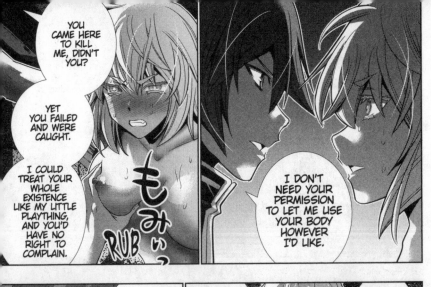

YOU CAME HERE TO KILL ME, DIDN'T YOU?

YET YOU FAILED AND WERE CAUGHT.

I COULD TREAT YOUR WHOLE EXISTENCE LIKE MY LITTLE PLAYTHING, AND YOU'D HAVE NO RIGHT TO COMPLAIN.

もみぃ RUB

I DON'T NEED YOUR PERMISSION TO LET ME USE YOUR BODY HOWEVER I'D LIKE.

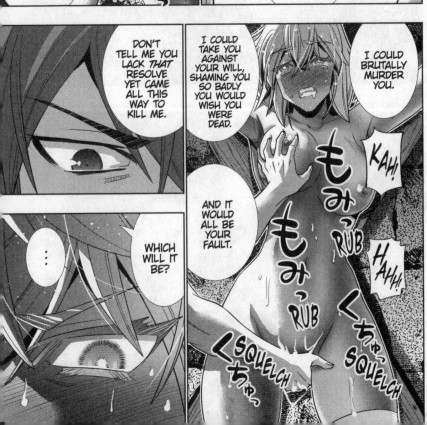

DON'T TELL ME YOU LACK *THAT* RESOLVE YET CAME ALL THIS WAY TO KILL ME.

I COULD TAKE YOU AGAINST YOUR WILL, SHAMING YOU SO BADLY YOU WOULD WISH YOU WERE DEAD.

I COULD BRUTALLY MURDER YOU.

AND IT WOULD ALL BE YOUR FAULT.

...

WHICH WILL IT BE?

もみぃ RUB

KAH!

もみぃ RUB

HAH!

くちゅ、SQUELCH

くちゅ、SQUELCH

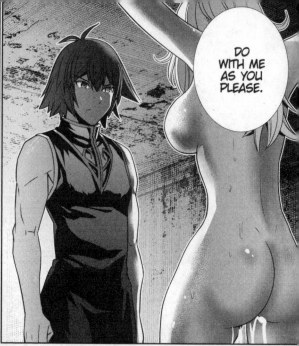

DO WITH ME AS YOU PLEASE.

THAT'S WHAT I THOUGHT.

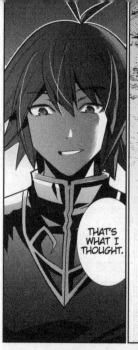

AND SOMEONE IS READY. YOU'RE OVERFLOWING WITH EXCITEMENT.

?!

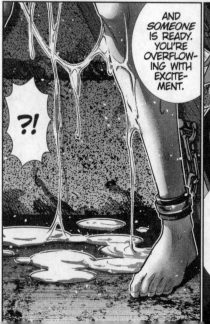

BUT I'M GLAD.

I'M A GENTLEMAN. IT'S NOT MY STYLE TO TAKE YOU BY FORCE.

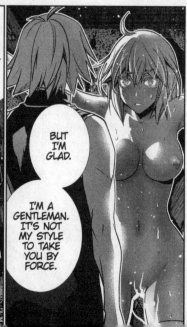

OHHH?

THERE IS NO WAY!!

QUIT MOCK- ING ME!!

!!!!!!!!!!!!!!

DESPITE BEING *THAT* TURNED ON OVER THE THOUGHT OF MATING WITH ME, YOU SURE ARE STUBBORN.

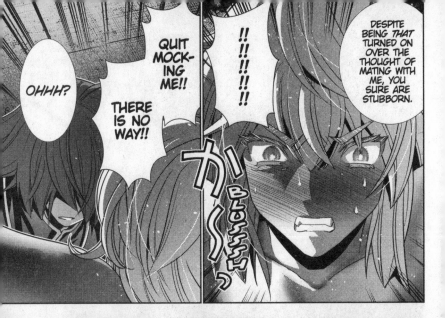

カッ

ブルルルル

FORCE YOURSELF ON ME IF YOU MUST!!

IF YOU WILL MATE WITH ME THEN DO AS YOU PLEASE!!

I TOLD YOU, I'M NOT LIKE THAT.

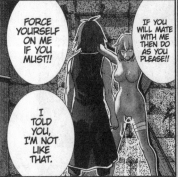

⋮

THEN WHAT IS THIS?!

ネチャ

STRETITCH

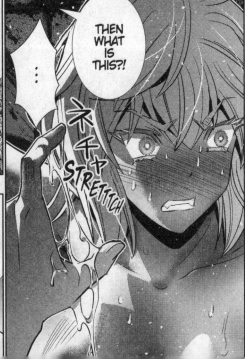

I WILL ONLY DO IT IF IT IS CONSEN- SUAL.

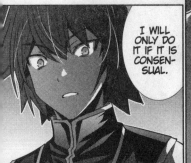

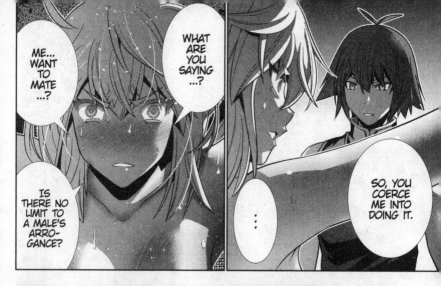

ME... WANT TO MATE...?

WHAT ARE YOU SAYING...?

IS THERE NO LIMIT TO A MALE'S ARROGANCE?

SO, YOU COERCE ME INTO DOING IT.

...

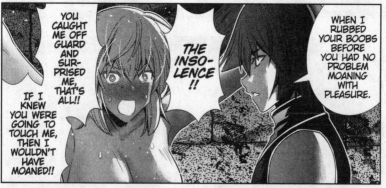

YOU CAUGHT ME OFF GUARD AND SURPRISED ME, THAT'S ALL!!

IF I KNEW YOU WERE GOING TO TOUCH ME, THEN I WOULDN'T HAVE MOANED!!

THE INSOLENCE!!

WHEN I RUBBED YOUR BOOBS BEFORE YOU HAD NO PROBLEM MOANING WITH PLEASURE.

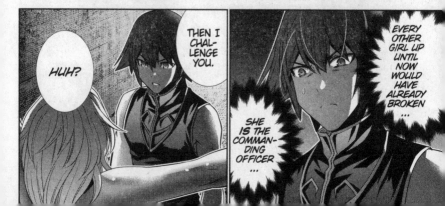

HUH?

THEN I CHALLENGE YOU.

EVERY OTHER GIRL UP UNTIL NOW WOULD HAVE ALREADY BROKEN...

SHE IS THE COMMANDING OFFICER...

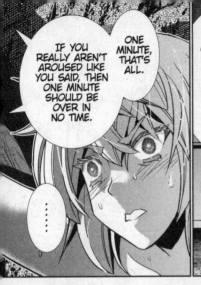

IF YOU REALLY AREN'T AROUSED LIKE YOU SAID, THEN ONE MINUTE SHOULD BE OVER IN NO TIME.

ONE MINUTE, THAT'S ALL.

......

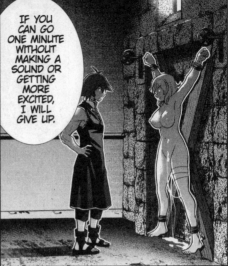

IF YOU CAN GO ONE MINUTE WITHOUT MAKING A SOUND OR GETTING MORE EXCITED, I WILL GIVE UP.

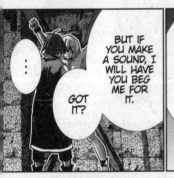

...

BUT IF YOU MAKE A SOUND, I WILL HAVE YOU BEG ME FOR IT.

GOT IT?

YOU WERE THE ONE WHO AGREED TO A ONE-ON-ONE FIGHT, DID YOU NOT?

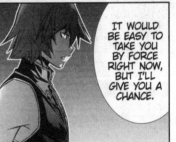

IT WOULD BE EASY TO TAKE YOU BY FORCE RIGHT NOW, BUT I'LL GIVE YOU A CHANCE.

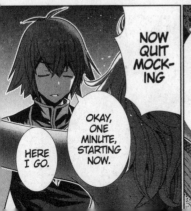

NOW QUIT MOCKING

OKAY, ONE MINUTE, STARTING NOW.

HERE I GO.

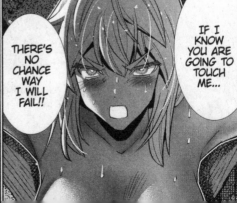

THERE'S NO CHANCE WAY I WILL FAIL!!

IF I KNOW YOU ARE GOING TO TOUCH ME...

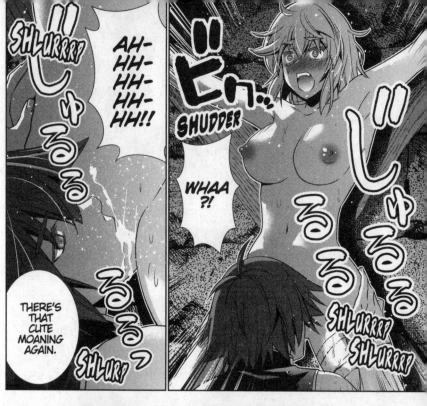

SHLURRRP

AH-HH-HH-HH-HH!!

ビn...

SHUDDER

WHAA?!

THERE'S THAT CUTE MOANING AGAIN.

SHLURRP

じゅるるる

SHLURRRP
SHLURRRP

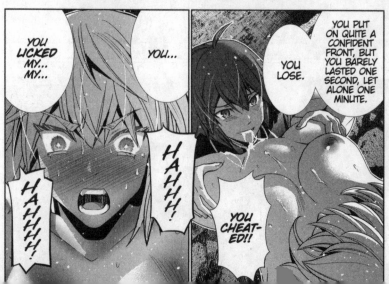

YOU LICKED MY... MY...

YOU...

YOU LOSE.

YOU PUT ON QUITE A CONFIDENT FRONT, BUT YOU BARELY LASTED ONE SECOND, LET ALONE ONE MINUTE.

HAHHH!

HAHHH!

YOU CHEATED!!

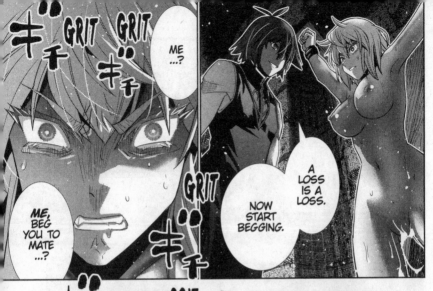

ME...?

GRIT GRIT

キチ キチ

A LOSS IS A LOSS.

NOW START BEGGING.

ME, BEG YOU TO MATE...?

GRIT

キチ

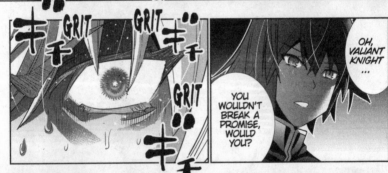

キチ GRIT GRIT キチ

GRIT

キチ

OH, VALIANT KNIGHT...

YOU WOULDN'T BREAK A PROMISE, WOULD YOU?

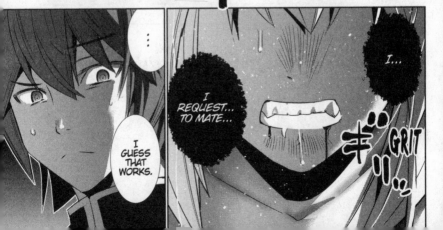

:

I GUESS THAT WORKS.

I REQUEST... TO MATE...

I...

キチ GRIT

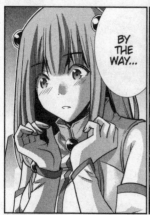

BY THE WAY...

YEAH.

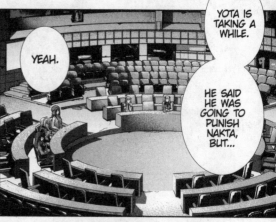

YOTA IS TAKING A WHILE.

HE SAID HE WAS GOING TO PUNISH NAKTA, BUT...

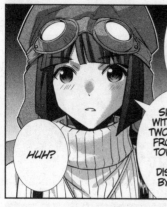

HUH?

LILIA SET OFF FOR MEESE TOWN A WHILE BACK.

SHE WAS WITH THOSE TWO SAILORS FROM REEL TOWN THAT WERE DISPLACED BY GALIA.

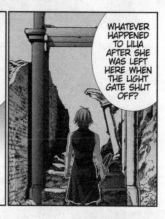

WHATEVER HAPPENED TO LILIA AFTER SHE WAS LEFT HERE WHEN THE LIGHT GATE SHUT OFF?

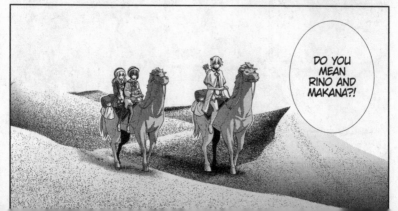

DO YOU MEAN RINO AND MAKANA?!

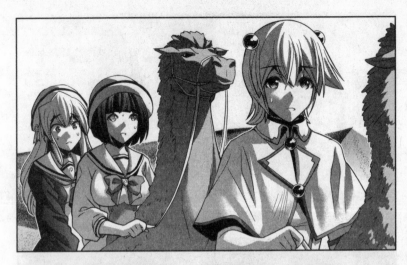

I SEE... THAT EXPLAINS WHY WE DIDN'T CROSS PATHS ON OUR WAY HERE.

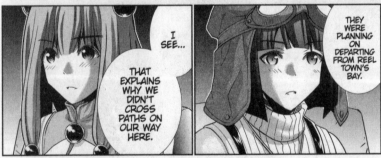

THEY WERE PLANNING ON DEPARTING FROM REEL TOWN'S BAY.

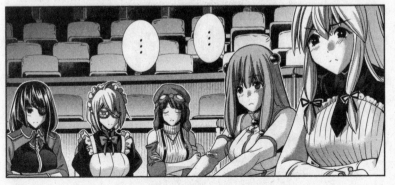

...

...

YOTA REALLY IS TAKING A LONG TIME...
I WONDER WHAT HE MEANT BY PUNISH?
COULD HE HAVE MEANT TORTURE ...?
HE SAID HE WAS GOING TO AROUSE HER AND THEN LEAVE HER BE.
HUH ?!
SHE MIGHT STILL BE AROUSED EVEN NOW.
...
...
THAT MUST BE PAINFUL.
NO KIDDING.

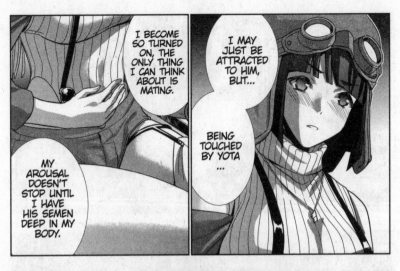

I BECOME SO TURNED ON, THE ONLY THING I CAN THINK ABOUT IS MATING.

I MAY JUST BE ATTRACTED TO HIM, BUT...

BEING TOUCHED BY YOTA...

MY AROUSAL DOESN'T STOP UNTIL I HAVE HIS SEMEN DEEP IN MY BODY.

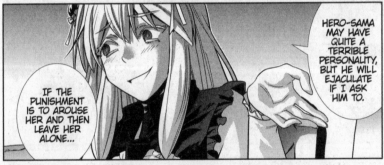

HERO-SAMA MAY HAVE QUITE A TERRIBLE PERSONALITY, BUT HE WILL EJACULATE IF I ASK HIM TO.

IF THE PUNISHMENT IS TO AROUSE HER AND THEN LEAVE HER ALONE...

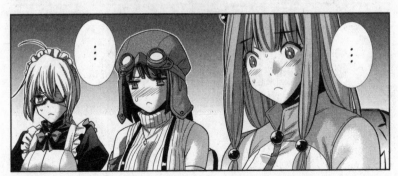

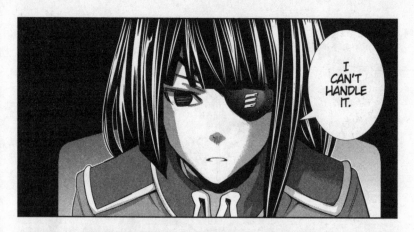

I CAN'T HANDLE IT.

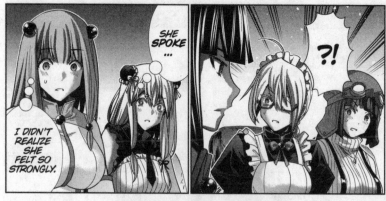

SHE SPOKE...

I DIDN'T REALIZE SHE FELT SO STRONGLY.

?!

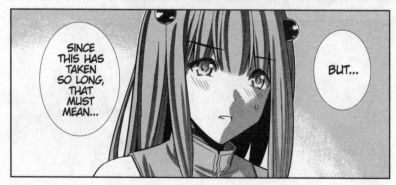

SINCE THIS HAS TAKEN SO LONG, THAT MUST MEAN...

BUT...

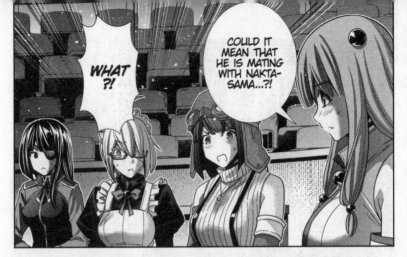

WHAT ?!

COULD IT MEAN THAT HE IS MATING WITH NAKTA-SAMA...?!

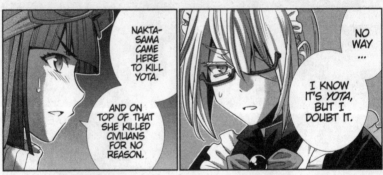

NAKTA-SAMA CAME HERE TO KILL YOTA.

AND ON TOP OF THAT SHE KILLED CIVILIANS FOR NO REASON.

NO WAY ...

I KNOW IT'S *YOTA*, BUT I DOUBT IT.

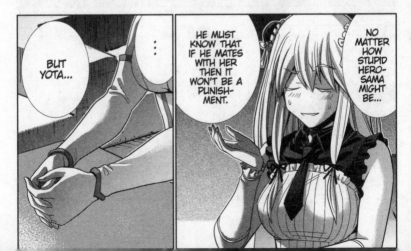

:

BUT YOTA...

HE MUST KNOW THAT IF HE MATES WITH HER THEN IT WON'T BE A PUNISH- MENT.

NO MATTER HOW STUPID HERO-SAMA MIGHT BE...

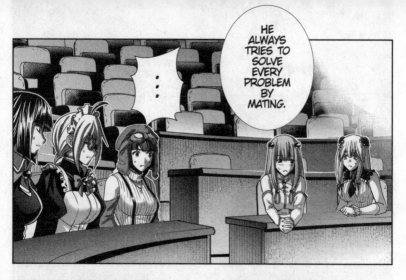

HE ALWAYS TRIES TO SOLVE EVERY PROBLEM BY MATING.

⋯

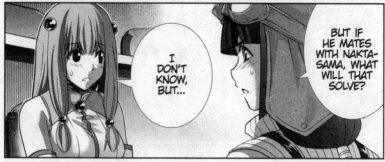

BUT IF HE MATES WITH NAKTA-SAMA, WHAT WILL THAT SOLVE?

I DON'T KNOW, BUT...

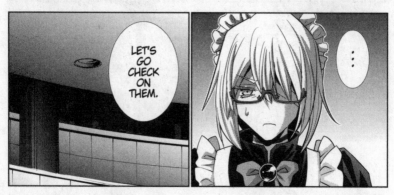

LET'S GO CHECK ON THEM.

⋯

カチャ
KER-CHAK
AHHHHHH!!
?!
AHHHHH!!
パン
SHLAP
パン
SHLAP
AHHHHH!!
パン
SHLAP

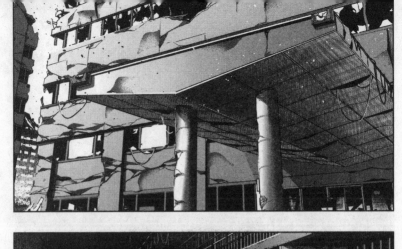

AHHHHHHHHH!
SHLAP
SHLAP
SHLAP
SHPLURT
SHLAP
SHLAP
SHPLURT
AHHHH!!
WHAT ...?!

PARALLEL
PARADISE

NEXT
I WON'T COME!!
I SWEAR I WON'T!!
SHLAP
THE IMPREGNABLE FEMALE KNIGHT, NAKTA...
SHPLURT
AH-HH-HH!
HAS BEEN BESTED BY A MALE?!